MAGOG
1982
CANCELED

MAGOG 1982 CANCELED

by
David Allen Lewis

New Leaf 🍃 Press
Box 1045, Harrison, Ark. 72601

First Printing, October 1982

Typesetting by Type-O-Graphics
Springfield, MO 65806

Library of Congress Catalog Card Number: 82-62079

International Standard Book Number: 0-89221-103-2

CONTENTS

PREFACE

Here are some of the almost unknown facts about the Israel-PLO-Lebanon war of 1982. They are not unknown because they are unknowable, but because for some reason the Western press has remained almost silent on some of the most important aspects of the conflict.

We can say that Israel's action, far beyond being a strike against terrorism, actually prevented the Russian takeover of the oil rich Middle East and/or the dreaded third world war. If Russia ever takes control of the Middle East it will bring the West to its knees and provoke the worst economic depression of all history.

It may be, in the final analysis, that far from being Israel's protector, the United States of America will be seen as having been saved from ruin by Israel. Actually, the relationship between these two countries is the bulwark of freedom for the entire Western world. How vital it is for our people to know the real facts behind the recent events in the Middle East.

Many religious people have understood the prophecies of Ezekiel (chapters 38, 39) to be a prediction of a future invasion of Israel by Russia and her allies. The desired outcome of the battle is a Soviet takeover of the entire Middle East.

The interpretation of Gog of the land of Magog being Russia and her final ruler is a very old idea. The lexicography of *Gesenius* published in 1812, identifies Magog as Russia long before Russia became a significant world power. Flavius Josephus, contemporary of Jesus, wrote of Sythian tribes who in ancient times settled north of the Caucasus Mountains (in present-day Russia). He said they were tribes of Magog or the Magogites.

Outstanding media evangelists such as Jim Bakker and Pat Robertson have called the attention of millions to these curious predictions. Guests on various religious talk shows have been even more bold in declaring that the Russian invasion of the Middle East is very near at hand.

As a matter of fact, Pat Robertson, host of the 700-Club TV show went so far as to say that he felt it would take place this year (1982). In a paper Robertson publishes (*Pat Robertson's Perspective*), he showed keen insight by saying, "It is almost certain that Israel will attempt to preserve its interests by striking against Southern Lebanon and Syria. This in turn could bring the Iranians and their Soviet allies to move directly against Israel" (*Perspective*, April 1982). The February 1982 *Perspective* had Robertson's prediction that Russia would attack Israel. He said, "The onrush of events toward the end of the year may see the world in flames. Remember that these events are clearly foretold by the prophet Ezekiel."

In the summer 1982 edition of *Perspective* Robertson again wears the prophets mantel as he says, "When the reprisal comes it will fulfill the prophecy of the prophet Ezekiel, who in the 38th chapter foretold an invasion of Israel in the 'latter days' of Russia, Iran, Ethiopia, and Libya. That invasion . . . is very near . . . possibly as near as the fall of this year (1982)." We believe that Israel's action in Lebanon has CANCELED MAGOG 1982.

Venerable orthodox rabbis in Israel have been reported as predicting a Russian invasion, based on dreams and visions given to them. They have prophesied of Russia coming like a storm into Israel and being defeated by the intervention of the Almighty.

There are various opinions as to when the Magog invasion will take place in relation to other end-time events in Biblical prophecy. Some theologians see the possibility of the Russian invasion taking place momentarily. Others, believing in a "pre-tribulation rapture" say that it must take place during the great seven-year global trauma, the tribulation. Eschatologists are agreed, however, that Magog's invasion sets off the global conflict that culminates in the battle of Armageddon.

The prophet Ezekiel is adamant in declaring that Israel, because of God's intervention, will be triumphant over Magog.

The very fact that honest scholars differ in opinion on the timing of the Magog invasion (in relation to the other prophesied events) may indicate that the prophecy is open-ended. That is, depending on many factors God may allow the battle to take place at one time, or if other factors prevail, based on human action, the battle could take place at another time in relationship to the end-time scenario.

Today's mail brought more interesting documentation from Dr. Lambert Dolphin, senior research physicist with SRI INTERNATIONAL (formerly Stanford Research Institute), in Menlo Park, California, one of our nations major "think tanks." In a recent visit with Lambert at SRI my mind was staggered at the immensity of what is being done there. Lambert is a devout evangelic Christian, a rarity in his circles. Today this outstanding scientist wrote:

> "I know you have been sharing with us here the stress and strain and uncertainty of recent months centering around the Middle East.
>
> We are probably too close in time to the tumultuous changes in and around Israel this summer, but in talking yesterday with Ray Stedman I was interested to hear him say he felt we may have narrowly missed the rapture, the Russian invasion and the escalation of end-time events because of a last minute change of divine plans for some as yet unknown reason.
>
> Ray believes, as I do as well, that the responses of God's people affect the countdown of prophecy and that we have just gone through a 'joint or articulation' in time that in effect has moved the return of the Lord downstream a bit further. This means, of course, that a delay in our project and thus the building of the Third Temple is appropriate.
>
> After Chuck Smith's tour of Israel early in the year I promptly sent Stanley Goldfoot Chuck's tape PROPHECY 1982 and PROPHECY UPDATE."

Goldfoot, a Jewish man, heads up the Temple Foundation of Jerusalem and is a leader in the endeavor to rebuild the Temple of Israel on Mount Moriah.

Lambert added: "I now believe Stanley circulated these tapes widely in Israeli government circles giving them additional warning of an imminent invasion from the North. This in turn helped them to decide to invade Lebanon where they captured $2 billion in sophisticated Russian weaponry and delayed any Syrian-PLO attack on Israel from the North by months or possibly years, delaying therefore Ezekiel 38, 39."

Dr. Lambert Dolphin is a careful research scientist and not given to rash statements. His mention of $2 billion of SOPHISTICATED RUSSIAN ARMAMENTS found by the Israelis in South Lebanon is a valuable confirmation of what you will find in this book *MAGOG 1982/CANCELED*. Do you have any idea what $2 billion buys in armaments? It is our opinion that this book will have a stunning impact on people's thinking concerning the recent Mideast conflict.

Dr. L. Dolphin said: "Israel is a tiny country. Mr. Begin holds Bible studies in his home every Sabbath and receives a host of Christian visitors constantly. He is certainly therefore exposed to and influenced by Christian eschatological thought."

I have personally discussed the Ezekiel 38 passage with Prime Minister Menachem Begin, and I know that Rev. Hilton Sutton has met with Begin's advisors, shown them films, and done a presentation for them on the Gog and Magog (Russia) passage. Sutton's presentation (for which I acted as an advisor) was called "THE EZEKIEL FILE."

"Thus, I believe that all your actions," wrote Lambert, "and ours are playing an exciting and interesting role in the destiny of Israel. The Jewish Jerusalem City treasurer told me in January that one must be very careful what one does in Jerusalem—'We are all so close to God here, whether Jew or Moslem or Christian. Every move we make sends ripples around the world.'"

The prophet Zechariah said that in the end times Jerusalem would be a cup of trembling. This raises an interesting speculation. Are we living in the days the ancient Hebrew seers foretold? How close were we to the actual beginning of World War III in 1982? Did Russia have plans for a massive PLO-fronted invasion of Israel set to take place on August 4, 1982? Did Israel's invasion of Lebanon cancel Magog 1982? Are we being given an extended period of grace? If so, what is the desire of Almighty God for humanity during the period of time that lies ahead? What should you be doing about His ongoing plan and purpose?

—David A. Lewis
Springfield, MO
October 1982

1

DID ISRAEL PREVENT THE THIRD WORLD WAR?

Israel's invasion of Lebanon freed north Israel from the constant threat of PLO terrorism. It served to liberate the Lebanese people; but far beyond these significant accomplishments it can now be said that in all likelihood Israel's action saved the world from:
- Russian takeover of the Mideast
- Resultant massive economic depression in the Western world
- Third World War

While the press is casting Israel in the role of villain, we believe that the above concept can be demonstrated.

Just before going to Lebanon recently to see the situation firsthand and to talk to the Lebanese people, we received a xerox copy of an intelligence report that appeared in the July 28, 1982 edition of *Review of the News*. I called *Review of the News* to check further on the authenticity of this bizarre report that seemed almost unbelievable. They simply said that the reporter, a Mr. H. du Berrier who filed the report was totally reliable. Since then I have talked to an ordained minister (whom I have known for some time) from Utah who claims to know du Berrier, also confirming that the man is a careful and accurate reporter. At the present time we

11

are trying to locate and interview duBerrier. Independent sources of information, including an interview with a US government official who works for one of President Ronald Reagan's cabinet members, and information directly from Asher Naim of the Israeli Foreign Ministry, Jerusalem, confirm the accuracy of the report. Here is the du Berrier intelligence report:

INTELLIGENCE FROM LEBANON

It would be wrong to think of the Israeli BLITZKRIEG into Lebanon and the seemingly hopeless predicament of Yasir Arafat's encircled Palestine Liberation Organization (PLO) as creating a prelude to peace in the Middle East. From unimpeachable information reaching your correspondent, it is clear that what we are seeing now is only the beginning of a struggle which could make the word holocaust seem an understatement.

From November 13, 1979, when Yasir Arafat sat down in the Kremlin with Soviet Foreign Minister Andrei Gromyko, major conflict in the Middle East was in the works. Arafat had gone to Moscow with a clear-cut proposal. "Comrade Gromyko," the Palestinian leader said, "I have only hand-held weapons with which to confront the Israelis to whom the Americans have given their most sophisticated arms. Even the Polisario Front has been armed with Russian missiles for its war with Morocco. Yet that struggle, compared to ours, which in the ultimate reckoning is against the Americans, is of little importance to you. Can't you see that by arming us you are fighting the Americans? I propose that we make common cause."

Andrei Gromyko listened sympathetically and agreed to bring the matter before a meeting of Politburo and Red Army leaders. Before Yasir Arafat left Moscow the promised discussions were under way. The Soviet military was all for taking up Mr. Arafat's proposition on grounds that the PLO was a force already created, filled with hate, and ready to accept any risk. Using that group as an entering wedge, the Soviets could make Lebanon a springboard for an offensive against the oil-laden Arabian peninsula.

But the Soviet politicians were reluctant. The two most effective intelligence networks in the world are Israel's Mossad and Moscow's K.G.B. Mossad was built up with religion as a catalyst and has spread its operations across the globe in the service of a religious state. The K.G.B. is political, with class struggle as a crystalizing agent and Moscow as its Vatican. At times, when Israel was under Labor Governments, the interests of the two agencies have overlapped. For Moscow to commit herself to the Palestinian cause, however, would mean all-out war between these competing agencies.

In the end the thinking of the Soviet military won out and Moscow decided to join with the PLO and shoot the works for the greater stakes. Not a moment was lost. Planning started immediately and what the Palestinians and Soviets together have accomplished since that November 1979 meeting defies imagination. Lebanon was made the pivot for Moscow's plans for conquest of the Middle East. Around the village of Saida the largest secret military base was tunneled out. Steel reinforced caverns and miles of underground galleries were cut through earth and rock to link huge command and storage halls, some of them large enough to shelter fleets of helicopters . . .

One chamber comprised a vast intelligence storehouse loaded to the ceiling with methodically arranged files. Dossiers on thousands of individuals lined one wall. Rows of shelves held military plans for every conceivable operation and region. A map section covered land areas, ports, and sea bottoms of the world. Significantly, all of the captured documents were in Russian . . .

The names and records of all Soviet advisors in Lebanon were found in files dating back to the beginning of Soviet/PLO cooperation. Already Mossad has the names of more than 2,000 Europeans and Americans in the Palestinian "foreign legion" along with a library of documentation on terrorists working on the European and American continents under directions from Moscow. More alarming, enough missiles, cannons, tanks, and other armored vehicles to equip a modern army were turned up in the underground depot. A special radar and electronic communications system occupied a self-contained wing of the complex.

Another unexpected discovery in the Soviet fortress beneath Saida was files listing important Western firms and personalities who for one reason or another—including blackmail—have been supporting the Palestinian cause politically and financially. Many turned out to be American.

What Western military leaders should start thinking about immediately is the extent to which the uncovering of the Palestinian burrows constitutes a military defeat for the Soviet Union. This opens the possibility that the Mossad's agents had warned Tel Aviv of the base and plans for a Soviet action to be set in motion this August. If so, that could have decided the date for launching the present Israeli invasion of Lebanon.

A greater unknown remains—one that might be settled before this report is published: considering the importance of the documents Mossad technicians are amassing as one strong room after another is opened, the Israelis had to consider the possibility of Moscow taking action to save the Palestinians in Beirut. European intelligence experts began asking themselves if this was the explanation for Yasir Arafat's cockiness as he refused offers of safe-conduct and evacuation, though cut off from every avenue of escape. —H. DU B.

As you read the last paragraph remember that this was published the 28th of July and filed somewhat earlier. In retrospect we can see that Israel's successes stopped the evil plans of the Soviets and now Arafat and most of the PLO terrorists have exited Beirut.

Here are questions I asked Mr. Asher Naim, director of the Information Division of the Israeli Foreign Ministry:

LEWIS: "We have been reading reports of a huge underground base that has been discovered in Saida (Sidon). Is that correct?"

ASHER NAIM: "That is true. That is correct."

LEWIS: "I have some of that report here: 'Lebanon was made the pivot for Moscow's plans for the conquest of the ENTIRE MIDDLE EAST. Around the village of Saida the largest SECRET MILITARY BASE in the world was tunneled out . . . steel reinforced caverns . . . MILES of underground galleries . . . fleets of helicopters . . . ultra secret chambers . . . steel doors that could only be opened by emissions by radio waves from submarines.' IS THIS ACCURATE?"

ASHER NAIM: "Well, what we found near Saida, and not only in Saida—tunnels that can puzzle your mind—about the length of it—I wouldn't believe it. I mean even we with our good intelligence . . . we pride ourselves in our good intelligence, we were puzzled. Even our intelligence was surprised about the magnitude of it. We knew there was a bunker here, a bunker there, but we never saw until this war that the bunkers can be turned into a whole tunnel where you can go hundreds of yards. They are filled up with equipment of all sorts of all products. And that is why we were puzzled. For whom is this being stored? Who is going to use it? Are they going to be used by someone else who will come from across the sea?"

LEWIS: "What about the documents? Storerooms of documents, also?"

ASHER NAIM: "That is right. Now we found much, much material."

LEWIS: "Documents?"

ASHER NAIM: "Documents, that we are now day in and day out—you could fill up whole rooms—and we are going to find out exactly what all these documents ultimately mean."

Mr. Naim shared a volume of other information which will be referred to later. From an outside and official source, this was my first real authentication of the report printed in this chapter.

I asked a lot of other people in Israel about this but got noncommittal answers. One military officer said, "Look, Lewis, nobody is going to confirm or deny this information. It is something we have not fully evaluated. The whole truth may never be told to the public. There is a lot of international pressure being exercised." Another officer told me that the whole world could just thank Israel for preventing a Russian-backed invasion of the entire Mideast, and for stopping the third world war. He added that there was enough armaments in Lebanon to furnish an army of 500,000 men. Since there were only about 19,000 PLO fighters in Lebanon, one wonders who was to comprise this army. We do know that men from eleven different countries were discovered in the PLO ranks. Others told me that the plan was to use troops from Africa, various Mideast countries, Eastern European nations, and Russia to come in and form this massive army. Since then I have heard from two sources that the armaments would furnish an army of about one million men. More accurate figures will probably be forthcoming in weeks to come.

Very early in the war the following report was filed by Media Analysis Center. Remember, this is a very early report (June 30). Much more has come to light since this report was given.

THE U.S.S.R.—PLO CONNECTION

The 4,000 tons of ammunition transferred (as of June 30, 1982) from PLO bunkers in South Lebanon, and the huge quantity of light and heavy armaments seized from the PLO, raise the possibility that these stocks—in addition to the ammunition and armaments still under the control of the PLO—have been intended not only as prepositioned weaponry against Israel, but also as a prepositioned stock used by Soviet-designed international terrorism against Western targets.

That possibility gains considerable ground in light of the sizeable presence in Lebanon of international terrorists as evidenced by documents and terrorists seized by Israel. Furthermore, the presence in PLO camps of 620 members of the Italian Red Brigade, 153 of the West German Beider Meinhoff, 8,000 Turkish Terrorists, etc. (as reported on January 13, 1982 by the Phalangist Radio) constituted a major by-product of the USSR-PLO connection which benefited from (and further contributed to) the unique fragmentation and lack of sovereignty in Lebanon.

While many observers hastily discard Soviet commitment to the PLO and undermine the PLO's appreciation of the Soviets; and while it is obvious that the Soviets have never considered the PLO to be a central factor in their own Mideast policy; still the Soviet military assistance to the PLO has gone beyond the mere supply of arms. According to a PLO-Syria strategic working-paper signed on April 28, 1982 in Damascus, and discussed on April 30, 1982 by the Lebanese AL-ACHRAR (an organ of Chamoun's National Liberals), there were 21 Soviet, Cuban and East German military advisers, headed by a colonel, in major PLO camps in Sidon, Damor and Sabra (Beirut).

As a matter of fact, those who predict a PLO shift away from the USSR, are advised to examine the PLO's reaction to the USSR's inaction at the time of its two previous disasters—in (Black) September 1970 when the PLO was ruthlessly slaughtered and evicted from Jordan; and in April 1976 when the Syrian guns were responsible for the killing of 5,000 members of the PLO and for its eviction from its major headquarters in Beirut's Tel-Za'atar (which was totally demolished).

Despite the relative disappointment felt by the PLO, and despite the consistent courtship of the PLO on the part of West Europe and the United States (particularly during Carter's Administration), the PLO considered the USSR an INDIS-PENSABLE ALLY. That dependency on Moscow has been the natural by-product of the realization that it is only the Soviets who may be willing—for the sake of their own interests—to advance the ideology and the long-term objects of the PLO vis-a-vis Israel (while the West may be used by the PLO to contribute towards these objects). Also, only the Soviets may be relied upon by the PLO in the context of the PLO's inter-Arab position (especially, in view of its potential threat over pro-Western Arab leaders). Moreover, when it comes to seeking a long-term alternative operation base—compatible with the inherent substance and ideology of the PLO—it is the pro-Soviet Arab countries which come to mind (Syria, Libya, Algeria, South Yemen). Finally, it has been the PLO alliance with the Third World, and particularly with the anti-Western Third World leaders, which has further solidified its dependency upon Moscow.

That the scope of the USSR-PLO connection has gone beyond the military aspect is evidenced from Fatah documents seized by Israel. For instance, the document detailing an April 14-19, 1982 visit by a top Fatah delegation to East Germany indicates that the basis for the training sessions conducted in East Germany for Fatah members is the Marxist-Leninist doctrine. In addition to military-oriented courses, states the document, the trainees undergo political education, and study sociology and political science. Another document, seized in the PLO Democratic Front's headquarters lists East Germany, Czechoslovakia, Bulgaria, Rumania and the USSR as countries offering students scholarships in 1982.

The extent of the military ties between the PLO and Moscow—and the degree of pro-Soviet and anti-Western feelings characterizing the PLO—may be construed from the numerous lists of PLO graduates in military courses conducted in Soviet bloc countries including Vietnam, North Korea, Cuba, Hungary, East Germany, Bulgaria, Czechoslovakia, Poland and the USSR.

Predetermining the army-like quantity of the PLO weaponry located in South Lebanon were such reports as those by the Kuwaiti News Agency (February 5, 1982) on a shipment of SAM surface-to-air and GRAD surface-to-surface missiles and heavy artillery in the amount of $50 million, supplied to the PLO by Moscow; the PLO Radio (February 2, 1982) on FROG surface-to-surface missiles supplied by the USSR; and the West German DEUTSCHE TAGESPOST (November 11, 1981) on the supply of 30 T-54/55 tanks to the PLO by the Soviets.

List of PLO-Soviet Bloc Contacts (June 1982 - January 1982)

| June 29, 1982 | TASS | Yasser Abd Raba, member of the PLO executive, in Moscow |

26	French News Agency	Arafat meets Soviet Ambassador in Beirut, Soldatov, and receives a message from Brezhnev
26	Monte Carlo Radio	Arafat meets Yugoslav Ambassador
23	Monte Carlo Radio	Arafat meets Cuban Foreign Minister
18	Lebanese A-Sharq	Abu-Mazen, member of Fatah's Central Committee, to visit Moscow
11	Haddad's Radio	Arafat meets Soldatov
9	Beirut Radio	Kadumi, head of PLO's Political Department meets Gromyko in New York
4	PLO Radio	Arafat meets Soldatov
May 31	PLO Radio	Abu-Jihad, Arafat's deputy, meets delegation of the pro-Soviet Democratic Front for the Liberation of Somali
26	PLO Radio	Arafat meets Ceaucescu in Damascus
25	PLO Radio	Arafat meets Soldatov
20	PLO Radio	Arafat meets East German delegation
8	Saudi Al-Majallah	Arafat meets Soldatov twice during a week
8	Lebanese Al-Hadaf	Arafat meets Cuban delegation
6	PLO Radio	Arafat meets the head of the Soviet MidEast Inst.
5	Syrian News Agency	Khaled Al-Fahum, Chairman of the Palestine National Council, meets in Damascus the Chairman of the Bulgarian Assembly
1	Syrian Tishrin	1st PLO Ambassador to East Germany was accredited
April 30	Lebanese Al-Watan Al-Arabi	PLO may get improved SAM-7 and SAM-9
30	Lebanese Al-Achrar	21 Soviet, Cuban and E. German military advisors in PLO camps in Sidon, Damur and Sabra
30	TASS	Habash visits Moscow
27	PLO Radio	Arafat meets Soldatov
23	PLO Radio	Arafat and Abu-Jihad meet Soldatov
20	Syrian Al-Thawra	Khaled Al-Fahum meets Chairman of the E. German Assembly
16	Lebanese Al-Amam	Jibril, head of the Popular Front General Command, meets Soviet delegation
14	PLO Radio	High level PLO military delegation in East Germany
14	PLO Radio	Arafat meets Soldatov
13	Egyptian October	PLO members trained in Moscow operate in Salvador and Nicaragua
12	Libyan News Agency	PLO delegates in Vietnam and Sri-Lanka elevated to ambassadorial status
11	Lebanese A-Liwa	Talat Ya'akub, head of the Palestine Liberation Front, meets Soldatov
9	PLO Radio	Abu-Jafar, Kadumi's deputy, meets Soldatov
6	PLO Radio	Abu Jihad meets East German Ambassador
1	PLO Radio	Arafat meets Yugoslav Ambassador
March 28	Monte Carlo Radio	Hawatmeh, head of PLO's Dem. Popular Front, meets Castro in Havana
26	PLO Radio	Arafat meets Bulgarian delegation
22	Libyan News Agency	Abu-Maizer, PLO's spokesman, visits Moscow
16	Phalangist Radio	Arafat meets Soldatov
13	Iraq News Agency	Abu Mazen, member of Fatah's Central Committee, visits Moscow
13	Lebanese Amal	PLO delegation due to visit East Germany
11	Kuwait News Agency	Arafat in East Germany; increased military aid
9	Damascus Radio	Khaled Al-Fahum, Chairman of Palestine National Council meets a Czechoslovakian delegation
8/9	PLO Radio	Arafat meets Soldatov and Soviet Dept. Minister in charge of Cultural Affairs

3	PLO Radio	Arafat meets East German Ambassador
2	PLO Radio	Abu Jafar, Kadumi's deputy, meets North Korean Ambassador
February 21	PLO Radio	Abu Jihad, Arafat's deputy and head of PLO's military arm, welcomes delegation of the Bolivian revolutionary left
21	PLO Radio	Arafat meets Soldatov, the Soviet Ambassador in Beirut
18	PLO Radio	Abu Salah, member of Fatah Central Committee meets Soldatov
18	Syrian News Agency	Cooperation agreement signed between PLO and Bulgarian News Agencies
17	PLO Radio	Arafat meets Cuban and East German Ambassadors
16	PLO Radio	Pro-PLO rally in Prague
16	PLO Radio	Abu Jihad meets East German Ambassador
13	PLO Radio	Arafat, Abu-Jihad and Abu-Jafar meet Soldatov
12	Israel Davar	For the first time direct Soviet military supplies to the PLO
10	PLO Radio	Kadumi, head of PLO's political dept., meets East German Ambassador
5	PLO Radio	Arafat meets the Soviet attache in Beirut
4	PLO Radio	Arafat's talks in Hungary emphasize military assistance
2	PLO Radio	Soviet FROG missiles will be supplied to the PLO
2	PLO Radio	Abu Mazen welcomes Soviet delegation
1	Lebanese Al-Khuria	Hawatmeh welcomes delegation of the pro-Soviet Democratic Front for the Liberation of Somali
1	Kuwait News Agency	High PLO military delegation visited Moscow last week
January 31	PLO Radio	Arafat meets Soviet attache in Beirut
28	PLO Radio	Abu Jihad, head of the PLO military arm, meets defense and military VIPs in Belgrade and Prague
28	PLO Radio	Arafat meets Soviet attache
28	Phalangist Radio	Large Soviet military supplies
27	PLO Radio	Arafat and Abu Iyad welcome Soviet delegation
25	Lebanese Al-Hahar Al-Arabi	Kadumi signed military agreements in Cuba
22	PLO Radio	Economic agreement to be concluded between East Germany and the PLO
18	PLO Radio	Arafat visits Rumania
18	PLO Radio	Abu-Jihad and Abu Al-Walid, head of PLO's military operations, conduct military talks in Bulgaria
17	A-Liwa	Abu-Jihad and Abu Al-Walid conduct military talks in Hungary, USSR and Czechoslovakia
17	PLO Radio	Arafat and Kadumi meet Cuban Dep. Foreign Minister
17	French News Agency	Members of PLO's Central Committee visit Cambodia and Vietnam
15	Lebanese Al Safir	Talat Ya'akub, head of PLO's Palestine Liberation Front, visits Moscow
9	Lebanese Nidal Al-Shaab	Mahmud Al Mukhtar, member of the Popular Palestinian Struggle Front, visits Moscow
2	PLO Radio	Arafat meets Soviet attache in Beirut

The above from, The True Story: PLO Atrocities in Lebanon

Issued by the Information Department, Embassy of Israel, Washington, D.C. 20008

2

THE WASHINGTON REPORT

I talked at length with a U.S. government official who works for one of President Reagan's cabinet members. The name of this man is being withheld (at his request) for security reasons. I will refer to this man as John (not his real name).

This gentlemen is well known to me. He spent some time in Lebanon reviewing the situation there. I consider his information to be accurate. Here is a part of our conversation:

LEWIS: "What do you think of this report?" (I had just read the *Review of the News* report to John. I asked about the underground tunnels.)

JOHN: "I have been there. I was there when the Israeli's were dismantling the steel factories . . . as big as any steel fabricating plant I have seen in this country . . . this is where they were making the steel plates to use in the tunnels."

LEWIS: "Israel may have prevented the third world war and the takeover of the Mideast by Russia."

JOHN: "That is exactly what I was told by a member of MOSSAD (Israel's secret service) . . . that they prevented the third world war ... they found enough weapons to arm one million soldiers. I was told by this person in MOSSAD, and I have it in documentation ... that I got straight from the IDF (Israel Defense Forces) and the foreign ministry. I have pictures of some of the Russian language documents."

LEWIS: "Did you hear anything about the miles of underground galleries?"

JOHN: "Yes."

LEWIS: "You feel that that is true?"

JOHN: "Yes."

LEWIS: "What about documents in Russian?"

JOHN: "Right—look I took this stuff to the White House."

LEWIS: "Did you take it to ---?" (one of President Reagan's special advisors).

JOHN: "Yes."

LEWIS: "How did he react?"

JOHN: "--- told me that he knew that the State Department had some of this stuff. But he heard that the stuff they had, they had not delivered to the President."

LEWIS: "I wonder why?"

JOHN: "Because I know Ronald Reagan. All hell would break loose—that is my opinion. The State Department is dominated by Arab interests. They do not want Reagan to know the whole story."

In a later conversation with "John" the following significant information was shared:

LEWIS: "What do you think will come of the Syrian presence in Israel?"

JOHN: "Well, Syria will either get out or they will be at war with Israel. I had a strange feeling while I was over there that it isn't the last war. There could be another war real soon. The Russians might move in."

LEWIS: "I don't think Russia will move in the near future."

JOHN: "David, nothing would surprise me. The Russians have been dealt a severe blow. I know the Russian chief of air operations was in Damascus within three days after the Syrians' disastrous air losses. If you are just supplying a country with weapons, if you are nothing more than a salesman of arms, you don't send your chief of staff in to see what went wrong. If Israel had delayed sixty days it would have been too late. How does a nation of 2½ million (Israel) stand up against an army of a million men? I called Daniel (informant) in Israel today. He said that the people in Israel are in retrospect afraid because of what they found in Lebanon. They realize now what Russia intended. At this point 90% of the Israelis are in favor of the action that was taken. That is unheard of—such unprecedented support! The

The underground tunnel in Sidon crammed with vast quantities of arms and ammunition.

son of Moishe Dyan had been a big leader in the peace movement. After he visited Lebanon and they showed him what they found, he changed completely. He has turned completely around, and endorsed what Israel has done. Daniel also said he gives Saudi Arabia no more than two years. They will have an internal Khomeni-type revolution.

"There is a big fear in all the countries that are taking in the PLO. First of all the Arab regimes did not back the PLO in the current conflict. They didn't come to their aid—so the PLO is angry with them all. Now by letting the PLO come in they allow a viper into their own bosom. It is a theory that some of these regimes will render the PLO completely powerless for their own protection. Hussein (Jordan) might not be adverse to doing away with them. He tried to destroy them in 1970 when he drove them out of the country. Now they are going back to Jordan. There has got to be a lot of hostility there."

LEWIS: "Well, the whole situation is explosive."

JOHN: "David Pileggi (Israeli information officer) cites documents found in Lebanon that show that the PLO is interlinked with the terrorist groups worldwide. For example, the Turkish Popular Liberation Army, the Eritrian Liberation Front, the Japanese Red Army, the Secret Army for the Liberation of Armenia, the Argentinian Front, Brazilian Van Guardia, Chilean M.I.R., the Columbian Guerrilla Group, the Nicaraguan Sandanistas, the Guatemalian MR 13, the Uraguaian Tupamaros, Venezualian Carlos Network, the Italian Red Brigade, the Spanish Basque Binta, the Spanish ETA, the German Beider Meinhoff, the West German Red Army Faction, and the Irish Republican Army. These are groups that the PLO interrelates and works with for world Marxist revolution."

PROFESSOR NETANAYAHU SPEAKS

I sat for several hours with Professor Benjamin Netanayahu in Jerusalem discussing the inter-cooperation of the terrorist groups of the world. Perhaps no one in the world has better understanding than this man who heads the Jonathan Institute for the Research of International Terrorism. Netanayahu clearly spelled out that the "liberation" groups were not so interested (by the admission of some of their leaders) in national liberation as they were in world change and Marxist world revolution (communism).

ANOTHER CONVERSATION WITH "JOHN"

LEWIS: "John, since I talked to you last we have gotten more confirmation of the report on the Russian installations in Lebanon."

JOHN: "Well, the report is true, but there is a lot of information there that neither the Israelis or the Americans, or anyone else wants made public."

LEWIS: "As I told you, Asher Naim essentially confirmed the report."

JOHN: "Did he tell you that there was a date set for the beginning of the invasion against Israel? Further, a date was set for PLO-sponsored international hostilities. What it amounted to was that the Russians were using the terrorists to do their dirty work. How many files did your report say there were on terrorists in North America?"

LEWIS: "2,000 Moscow and PLO-operated agents in Europe and America."

JOHN: "More like 12,000 according to my information. The number one target, other than Israel, was Canada."

LEWIS: "What?"

JOHN: "Canada—and the number two target was the United States of America."

LEWIS: "Why Canada?"

JOHN: "Since the 1950's the French Military has been infiltrated by the communists. A lot of these people have worked their way into Canada, you know the French-Canadian Liberation Movement. Many of them are there now—trained, communist, past-French Military people. That's where their biggest group of volunteers and allies are.

This month (August 1982) the attack was to come on Israel with, the way the guy put it to me, was that the terrorist activity that was to begin in this country would make the Beider Meinhoff gang look like a bunch of pansies."

LEWIS: "This was to be in Israel and where else?"

JOHN: "Here in the USA, and other Western nations. Complete terrorist activity—neutralizing of power and water sources. Urban guerrilla warfare—actually the third world war. A conventional World War Three."

LEWIS: "Incredible."

JOHN: "Well, MOSSAD was really embarrassed. They found a thousand percent more than they dreamed possible in Lebanon. I just talked to my man Daniel in Jerusalem again. It was on the basis of the information MOSSAD did have that the invasion was made. It had to be. Daniel is sending me a complete set of photographs of the tunnel network. There was a movie produced by the IDF showing the findings in Sidon and all South Lebanon. It has been shown to over a hundred journalists and not one has mentioned it."

RUSSIAN LANGUAGE DOCUMENTS IN LEBANON

"John" read translations of many Russian language documents to me, and showed me many of them. Many of these were graduation certificates issued to Palestinian terrorists who had gotten their training in Russia, Vietnam, Bulgaria, East Germany, India, China, etc. One of tens of thousands of Russian language certificates found in Lebanon:

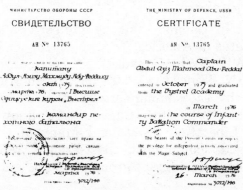

LEWIS: "Where did you get documentation on the tunnel system of the underground Russian installations in South Lebanon?"

JOHN: "I saw them. I was there."

Our informant then read extensively from translations of Arab and Russian language documents indicating the plans for the invasion and takeover of Israel.

LEWIS: "Israel's actions saved our nation from disaster as well."

JOHN: "You see, David, I used to believe, before I went over there, that the survival of Israel depended on us—on the USA and what we did. Now I see that it is exactly the opposite. Unfortunately very few people in this country of the USA know or appreciate that fact. Israel saved the whole world from a terrible blood bath."

CONFIRMATION KEEPS COMING

Today the mail brought more information and confirmation of the "intelligence report." Gideon Patt, Israeli Minister of Industry and Commerce made some open statements in a press interview in London. He reiterated what we had previously heard from several sources that while Israel's secret service (MOSSAD) was among the best in the world, even they, with their expertise were amazed at the findings in Southern Lebanon. He also revealed some new data which we had not previously heard or read.

Patt said, "We discovered a Russian-made machine which can drill a tunnel of 15 meters in diameter through solid rock in the mountains within a very short time."

Just think of a machine that can drill a tunnel through rock—fifteen meters (45 feet) in diameter!

Patt continued, "After hundreds of meters of one such tunnel we found arms from all over the Soviet bloc. There were some from Saudi Arabia, but the vast majority came from Eastern Europe, including Yugoslavia.

"Not only were there weapons in these tunnels for an army of 150,000— whereas the PLO had only some 15,000 men—but tents and blankets and food."

Remember that this interview was conducted in July, 1982. Since then many more installations have been found and some of our informants are talking about the possibility of arms being there for an army of a half million to a million men.

The Israeli official added, "We found 8,000 tons of coffee beans, which can be kept only for a limited period, because they deteriorate and have to be thrown into the sea."

This little item lends credibility to the idea that the Soviets really did plan an early-on invasion of Israel and the Mideast (August 4?).

Patt said,

> "Hidden, too, were 70,000 to 80,000 Kalashnikov rifles wrapped in oiled paper, thousands of rocket-propelled grenades, tens of thousands of shells, hundreds of Katyusha rockets and launchers and several SAM missile systems.

> "Seven hundred heavy trucks have been making their way every day to Lebanon from Israel to pick up the material, and it will take another sixty days before the task is completed.

> "The PLO leaders dreamed that within two years, the Syrians would have missiles over the skies of Galilee that would provide protection for the terrorists.

> "This 'missile umbrella,' they believed, would prevent the Israeli Air Force from intervening while the PLO established the base for a Palestinian State in Galilee."

> Even this strange illusion, Patt commented, could not explain the huge quantities of arms, a great proportion of them of the greatest sophistication, that were found stored in Southern Lebanon.

> "Some of these storage places were like ultra modern cinemas. One drove into air-conditioned tunnels, which had their own electric generators.

> "The PLO would have been incapable of building such

storage bases. Only the Americans, the Israelis or the Russians could have accomplished such a task. And no one has so far suggested that the Americans or the Israelis were involved.

BUILDUP STARTED IN 1979

"Moreover there are in Syria over 1,200 unmanned Russian tanks and a further 2,200 in Libya. And to bring into Lebanon 400 to 500 tanks would seem ridiculous if they were intended for the PLO.

"The build-up started at the end of 1979, after the signing of the Camp David accords. The Soviet Union used the entire Soviet bloc to send in equipment.

"Some 150,000 blankets arrived from North Korea, many thousands of Kalashnikov rifles from Bulgaria and Czechoslovakia, light ammunition from Yugoslavia, and SAM missiles from the Soviet Union.

"We in the Israeli Government were of the opinion that the Soviet Union would react in a very limited way to an Israeli move into Lebanon, because the Russians had told the Syrians: 'We are committed to help you and assist you within your own borders. What you do in Lebanon is your own business.' "

Patt talked about "top secret" PLO documents found in Lebanon. He told of Yasir Arafat's trips to Moscow, confirming what our Washington informant had said. Arafat conferred with high ranking Russian officials including Andrei Gromyko, Foreign Minister and Boris Ponomarev, head of the International Department of the Soviet Central Committee.

The Russians and Arafat discussed a PLO build-up in Lebanon and how the PLO could establish itself more strongly in the country without having to fear intervention by the Lebanese authorities. Gromyko remarked: "We have Syria on one side and you on the other."

Giving what he considered was the explanation for the enormous arms build-up in southern Lebanon, Patt said: "The Americans spoke about a vast strategic deployment in the Middle East. But even so, it would have taken the Americans four to five days to reach any emergency spot.

"If the Russians brought in 1,200 tanks in Syria and 2,200 tanks in Libya and huge supplies of weapons in southern Lebanon, they could fly two to three army divisions into the area immediately if a crisis developed.

"By the time the Americans arrived, the Russians would be in total control. The Russians do not trust the Iraqis and not even the Syrians."

Minister Patt expressed distress with the treatment the media had given Israel's position in the Lebanon action. On the other hand the media ignored PLO outrages.

He spoke of 12- and 13-year-old Lebanese girls that had been raped by the PLO men and were now pregnant.

A party of about thirty Syrian boys had arrived in Lebanon for a vacation trip. They were led as a tour group by their school teacher. The teacher decided to join the PLO, following which the boys were used to gratify the sexual demands of the terrorists.

The Israeli army boys found many bodies drained of blood in PLO hospitals. These people had been kidnapped in the streets and forced to give blood for the terrorists who had been wounded. Not a bit of blood was left in the bodies, which were thrown on the floor with the syringes still attached. Patt asked why the newspapers did not report these things when the facts were so easily available and so easily documented, both by photographs and the testimony of the Lebanese citizens who had observed these horrible activities.

I have been asked if President Ronald Reagan is acquainted with this information. I do not know. I do not think that he is. We have done our best to try and get the information to him. A letter dated August 28, 1982 was sent to President Reagan at the White House with a xerox of the original "intelligence report." The letter was also sent to the President in care of Secretary of the Interior, James Watt, with the request that he pass it on to President Reagan, if possible. A copy of the letter was sent to Morton Blackwell, special adviser to the President, with the same request. Did the information reach Mr. Reagan? I do not know.

Here is a copy of the letter sent to the President.

Dear Mr. President:

I hope the enclosed report reaches you. A gentleman who works for one of your cabinet members and myself have evidence that this report sent by Mr. H. duBerrier is correct. In fact there is a mass of evidence indicating that Israel's invasion of Lebanon has prevented the Russian takeover of the entire Mideast and/or a third world war.

Both the gentleman mentioned and myself have been in Lebanon recently.

Should you or any of your people require more information please call me (417-882-6470).

Sincerely,
David A. Lewis
President, National Christian
Leadership Conference for Israel

Your instincts in ultimately backing Israel have proven, thus, to be absolutely correct, and a blow against communism and international revolutionary terrorism has been struck. It has been suggested to me that there are those who do not want you to have a complete picture of what was going on in Lebanon before the Israeli invasion. All of our information is now available to you through and from many sources.

3

LEBANON IN CONFLICT
(a brief overview)

The land of Lebanon, north of Israel, was a model of democracy in the Arab world until 1975 and the outbreak of the civil war. Many Lebanese blame the presence of the PLO, and their agitation, for the start of that war. The country was about evenly divided between Moslem and Christian populations.

PLO finds a New Home
The Palestine Liberation (Terrorist) Organization was driven out of Jordan by King Hussein's armies in September, 1970. They had been such a disruptive force in Jordan that they could no longer be tolerated. The leadership moved to Lebanon late in 1970 and set up their operations there.

Terror Against Israel
Almost at once they started a campaign of terror against Israel. Everyone remembers the infamous bus massacre in 1971. How many people are aware, however that the PLO has NEVER attacked an Israeli military target—only soft civilian targets—women and children? On May 15, 1974 PLO terrorists attacked a school in Maalot, Israel, killing sixteen children and wounding seventy others. On April 11,

1974 the PLO attacked an apartment in Kiryat Shemona wounding sixteen and killing eighteen, including five women, eight children and five men. Over and over they fired Russian-made Katyusha rockets into the northern towns and villages of Israel. This is to say nothing of the multiplied atrocities committed against their own people and the Lebanese. Since the civil war in Lebanon began in 1975 over 100,000 lives have been lost as Arabs have fought Arabs. Lebanon has indeed become a land of tragedy. The Lebanese people tell us that as the PLO became a state within their country, the true Lebanese government became more and more destabilized. There are warring factions in Lebanon and the PLO used everything in their power to stir up trouble. This gave them a free hand to operate without the legitimate government cracking down on them.

Group of 56 Christian leaders in Jerusalem at briefing with Begin.

Syria's role in Lebanon

The Syrians have always claimed that they owned Lebanon. To them it is a part of "greater Syria." They have never established diplomatic relations with the legitimate Lebanese government. While the PLO made alliances with dissident groups, giving arms and training to them, the Syrians were getting ready to make their move. The civil war broke out in April 1975. I remember it well for I was in Beirut, Lebanon when the fighting raged in the streets. I had to hastily leave the country! All our missionaries who were based in Lebanon for the Mideast outreach soon had to leave the country.

In 1976 the Syrians moved in, claiming to be a "peace-keeping force." If ever there was a misnomer that is it. Syria has one simple aim and that is to conquer and own Lebanon as its own. Soon the Syrians controlled sixty percent of the country, and the PLO effectively controlled the rest. The situation changed as Major Saad Hadaad in the south of Lebanon raised up a true Lebanese liberation army to defend the people of south Lebanon from the PLO and the Syrians. I have met and talked to Major Hadaad in Metullah, in Israel, on the Lebanese border. I have talked to both Christian and Moslem Lebanese in the region. Did you know that the majority of Hadaad's "Christian" army is actually Moslem! With Hadaad in the south and the Maronite Christians in the north, about 20 percent of the country came back under legitimate Lebanese control. The PLO terrorism against the Lebanese and against Israel continued. For example all the people of the village of Damor in Lebanon were driven out by the PLO (after 1975).

SUPPOSE IT WAS HERE

What if a terrorist force camped in Mexico and regularly mounted attacks against the civilians of El Paso, Texas? What if they continually fired Katyusha rockets into that Texas city? It would not take the USA long to get a squadron of Marines across that border to clean out the terror group. Would we not be justified in doing that?

INVADORS OR LIBERATORS

Suppose those same terrorists were killing the Mexican people regularly. Suppose the Mexican government was being destroyed by their presence? Would the Mexican people greet the US Marines as foes or as liberators?

Israel invaded Lebanon, but the interesting thing is that in town after town the people met the Israelis in the streets with shouts of encouragement, as the allies were greeted in the liberation of France near the close of World War II. The Lebanese ran to the Jewish soldiers with cakes, cookies, cold drinks, rice and gifts. They sang and danced in the streets. This is no fantasy—it is confirmed by many independent observers. This was the reaction of Moslems as well as Christians in Lebanon. We sorrow with the Lebanese people over the civilian casualties. These casualty figures (not tens of thousands as first reported—the figure now is about three thousand casualties) would have been much lower if the PLO did not have the deliberate habit of putting its military installations right in the middle of civilian population centers. Many Christian and Jewish groups are now raising money for relief of the suffering Lebanese people.

4

ISRAEL AND LEBANON

An Israeli Document Dated April 22, 1982

Terrorist organizations whose centers, headquarters and bases are in Lebanon, have recently carried out murderous attacks against Israeli citizens both in Israel and in Europe. This reached a climax this morning when a terrorists' mine killed an IDF officer. In light of these blatant provocations, the government of Israel instructed the IDF to carry out a counterattack against three terrorist targets in Lebanon situated south of Beirut and northeast of Sidon.

The bombed targets had served as operational bases for terrorist attacks and sabotage against Israel. For many months, Israel acted with restraint in regard to the constant provocation of the PLO. Even after the murder in Paris of the Israeli diplomat, Yaacov Bar Simontov, Israel did not act. The government of Israel now expects the PLO to understand clearly that neither will Israel tolerate terror any more, nor disruptions of the cease-fire, nor any threats to its national security and civilian life.

Since 1976, Lebanon has virtually ceased to exist as an independent state. It is, in fact, a country occupied. The Syrian army, which invaded Lebanon on 1 June 1976 under the guise of an "Arab Deterrent Force," was never recalled, and today numbers some 27,000 troops. In effect, Lebanon has become a part of "Greater Syria."

Capitalizing on the absence of a strong central authority and encouraged by Syria, the PLO arrogated to itself *de facto* extraterritorial rights in its area of control extending from the Tyre bulge to the southern sections of Beirut. Currently, some 15,000 PLO terrorists are deployed in three main areas of Lebanon: some 6,000 are stationed in the "Syrian Zone," including Beirut where the PLO has established its headquarters in the midst of densely populated neighborhoods; some 8,000 are within the PLO dominated area; and about 700 are stationed in some 40 locations and strongholds in southern Lebanon in the area of operation of the United Nations Interim Force in Lebanon (UNIFIL). Since the beginning of their campaign of hostile attacks against Israel, the terrorists have used refugee camps or urban centers as bases of operation. Thus civilians were turned into human shields to provide the terrorists with immunity from attack.

For years the PLO terrorists used their military entrenchments in southern Lebanon as staging grounds for attacks against Israel across the Lebanese border. They also regularly attacked the Christian enclave—under the command of Major Saad Hadaad—which has steadfastly preserved some vestiges of Lebanese independence.

PLO SUBVERSION OF LEBANON

The boundary between Israel and Lebanon was peaceful up to 1968. At the end of that year, the PLO began to establish bases in South Lebanon. Because of its weakness, and under pressure from other Arab states, the Lebanese government was forced to allow the PLO a growing degree of freedom to operate within its territory.

The PLO "state within a state" became increasingly involved in the internal affairs of Lebanon. In addition to its bases within the refugee camps, the PLO established a network of organizational, training and logistical facilities in numerous Lebanese towns and villages. At the same time, the PLO increased the frequency and intensity of its attacks against Israel.

The encroachment of the PLO in Lebanon resulted in a radical polarization of Lebanese society, leading to the civil war which broke out in 1975 and to Syria's intervention the following year. By the fall of 1976, Lebanon had ceased to exist as a unified national entity.

Soon after, the PLO renewed its terrorist attacks against Israel from its bases in South Lebanon. They reached such a magnitude and intensity that in March 1978, the government of Israel had no choice but to mount Operation Litani—a military expedition into the south of Lebanon aimed at eradicating the PLO bases there and restoring security and normal life to northern Israel.

ROLE OF UNIFIL

In the wake of Operation Litani, the United Nations Security Council, by Resolutions 425 and 426 of 19 March 1978, instituted an interim UN force in Lebanon, charged with a three-fold mandate:

• *... of confirming the withdrawal of Israeli forces"* from southern Lebanon—completed June 1978, since Israel never intended remaining in the area;

• *... of restoring international peace and security and assisting the government of Lebanon in ensuring the return of its effective authority in the area"*—a goal which largely failed to materialize, as there has been virtually no central government control in Lebanon in recent years;

• *To insure that its* (UNIFIL's) *area of operation is not utilized for hostile activities of any kind"*—a goal also only partially fulfilled.

When Israel handed over to UNIFIL the area in southern Lebanon from which it had withdrawn, it was clear of terrorists. Israel fully expected that they would not be permitted to return to this area. However, Lebanon was still ruled, in effect, by Syria and the PLO, and terrorist bands returned to the south of Lebanon despite UNIFIL's presence and efforts.

The infiltration of the terrorists into the UNIFIL area took place gradually but steadily. They committed acts of sabotage against the population of South Lebanon and attempted to cross into Israel through the UNIFIL zone to attack Israel's border villages, sometimes attacking UNIFIL troops as well, resulting in 25 UNIFIL fatalities. However, when terrorist squads were intercepted by UNIFIL guards, they were escorted back out of the UNIFIL zone.

THE CHRISTIANS OF LEBANON AND ISRAEL JOIN IN OPPOSING PLO

Even more difficult was the situation of the population of South Lebanon who looked to Major Saad Hadaad for protection from the incessant attacks by PLO terrorists against them.

The Christians of Lebanon, once an equal partner in the country's democracy, were decimated and demoralized in the course of the civil war. The Syrians set out to break their remaining spirit and cruelly attacked them, including civilians. They became a weak minority without allies, abandoned by the West, cut off from their sources of supply, and unable to defend themselves and their territory. Israel provided the Christians with aid and support out of a sense of moral commitment, and to prevent the Syrian army from murdering their population unrestrained.

Israel had been providing humanitarian aid through the "Good Fence" to the population of South Lebanon since 1976. It began to extend its assistance in other ways as well, so that the area should not fall to the PLO and to prevent a Syrian military presence on Israel's border. The integrity of the enclave became a security and political asset for Israel. In fact, the enclave became a partner in Israel's war against the PLO forces.

ESCALATION OF ARMS SUPPLY TO THE PLO

In recent years the PLO concentrated on improving its capacity to reach Israeli civilian targets across the Lebanese border. This was achieved by an ever-increasing influx of long-range artillery, modern tanks, mobile rocket launchers, anti-aircraft missiles, etc.— supplied primarily by Libya, Syria and the Soviet Union.

On 15 May 1981, the PLO launched an intensive campaign of shelling Israeli villages and towns—extending all along Israel's northern frontier—which caused casualties and damage unprecedented since the 1973 Yom Kippur War. In July, the barrage of indiscriminate artillery and rocket attacks reached such an intensity that Israel had no choice but to take urgent measures to counter this mortal danger to its population. Only an Israeli strike at the PLO logistic and organizational infrastructure in Lebanon put an end to the PLO attacks.

JULY 1981 CEASE-FIRE IN LEBANON

On 24 July 1981, Israel responded positively to the proposal of United States Special Envoy Philip Habib, and agreed to the cessation of hostile activities on the Israel-Lebanon border. In doing so, Israel assumed considerable military risks because Syrian missiles continued to be emplaced in southern Lebanon, due to the fundamentally aggressive and violent nature of the PLO.

Israel's attitude towards this arrangement was expressed by Prime Minister Menachem Begin during a joint press conference with the late President Anwar Sadat in Alexandria on 26 August 1981, when he declared: *"I would like the cease-fire between Lebanon and Israel on the northern border of Israel to go on indefinitely."*

But Israel also made it very clear that Israel would defend itself if the terrorists broke the cease-fire by initiating hostile activities against any part of the Israeli-Lebanese border area.

As subsequent events proved, Israel's concern was well based.

RECENT ARMS ACQUISITIONS BY THE PLO IN LEBANON

Under the umbrella of the cease-fire, the PLO has meaningfully increased its military build-up. Immediately following the cessation of hostilities, the PLO ominously began receiving heavy armaments at an accelerated rate, primarily from Libya, Syria, Saudi Arabia, the Soviet Union and a number of eastern European countries. The PLO arsenal of artillery pieces in South Lebanon was increased to some 300 in recent months, more than three times as many as held previously.

The PLO also took advantage of the cease-fire to rehabilitate and reinforce its deployment in South Lebanon. Most of the command posts put out of action by the IDF were rebuilt, new approach roads constructed, additional telephone lines installed, and well-camouflaged arms and munition dumps established.

Since July 1981, the PLO launched or attempted to launch some 60 acts of terror; among these, three were against Hadaad's enclave, more than 20 from the Jordan border, and about 10 against targets in Europe. In addition, the PLO terrorists have continued their harassment of UNIFIL. Since the cease-fire went into effect terrorist forces attacked UNIFIL soldiers 63 times, wounding five.

PLO CALLED FOR CONTINUED ATTACKS AGAINST ISRAEL

Undeterred by the cease-fire, terrorist leaders continued to declare their intentions to attack Israel within its own territory and abroad.

The political editor of the terrorist *Voice of Palestine* declared on 30 July 1981:
"The cease-fire ... does not include an area outside of South Lebanon. ... It would be a big mistake to assume that we are speaking of a general cease-fire between the Palestinian revolution and the Zionist entity, or that this is a step in that direction. ..."

Abu Moussa, assistant to Fatah's operations commander, according to a terrorist broadcast from Lebanon on 24 July 1981, declared: "... *we clarify here that the cessation of bombardments is under no conditions a break in the armed struggle nor a pause in the continuation of the struggle against the Zionist entity.... The cessation of the shelling does not mean quiet.... The struggle continues in the occupied territory and in any place where the Zionist entity is located....*"

Farouk Kadoumi, head of the PLO political department, declared in an interview with the German weekly magazine *Stern,* according to *Radio Monte Carlo* and *Reuters* from Bonn on 28 July 1981: *"The Palestinians will continue to operate on the West Bank and the Gaza Strip, in spite of the cease-fire this past week on the Israel-Lebanon border ... we will never allow Israel to live in peace ... Even if the Palestinians achieve a state of their own on the West Bank and the Gaza Strip, the PLO will never recognize Israel."*

Despite all these PLO provocations in words and deeds, Israel demonstrated great restraint throughout.

CONCLUSION

In the period since the cease-fire went into effect, the PLO did not change its philosophy or its mode of operation. Its sole ambition remained the destruction of Israel by any possible means. Thus, any hopes that the cessation of hostilities to which Israel agreed would bring calm to the northern border and a halt to PLO terrorism were virtually destroyed in recent months. Once again, the actions and words of the PLO give the lie to any talk of moderation within the PLO.

Israel assumed great risks by agreeing on 24 July 1981, to suspend strikes against the PLO in Lebanon. There came a moment when Israel could not any longer accept the dangers generated by the PLO, as its bases in Lebanon exist solely for the purpose of harassing Israel's civilian population.

Israel supports the independence of Lebanon and its territorial integrity, and desires neighborly and peaceful relations with it. Israel does not have—and never had—any territorial claims against Lebanon.

Israel is vitally interested in peace in all of Lebanon. It seeks no military escalation or other deterioration of the situation. But it is the first and foremost duty of the Government of Israel to protect the lives and security of its citizens. The measures which the Israel Defense Forces were forced to adopt had one aim only: to ensure that the people of Israel—in their towns and villages—can lead normal and secure lives. Israel had no choice but to act, and will continue to take action in self-defense as long as terrorist attacks against its citizens continue. Action against the PLO is no diversion from the peace-making process, but a necessary, if grim, part of it.

Written in April, 1982, this material provides a clear warning of Israel's intentions. I obtained this information in Israel, but have lost identification of its source.

5

CHRISTIAN RESPONSE TO ISRAEL'S ACTION

In January, 1982 the Executive Committee of THE NATIONAL CHRISTIAN LEADERSHIP CONFERENCE FOR ISRAEL met in Berkeley, California. At that time I suggested that our next meeting, slated for June, 1982, be held in the nation's capitol. Further, I proposed that we do something visible in support of Israel. The committee unanimously accepted these proposals.

Rev. Renton Hunter graciously offered us the use of his church facilities for the June meeting. Hunter had stood with me in front of the White House on August 2, 1975, participating in a prayer demonstration for Israel. We bore a large banner that read: **CHRISTIANS UNITED FOR THE BIBLICAL RIGHT OF ISRAEL TO ITS LAND.**

Little did the committee realize in January that when we met in Washington in June that Israel would be involved in the Lebanon war. As we came together it was with a feeling that God had led us to the right place for such a time as this. The committee sat in session on June 14. I had been one of the original founders and incorporators of NCLCI, serving on the permanent board of directors and as chairman of the executive committee. In June I was elected to the presidency of the organization, succeeding Dr. Franklin Littell of Temple

University. Littell is author of *The Crucifixion of the Jews,*
and is now president emeritus of NCLCI.

MEETING IN LAFAYETTE PARK

On the fifteenth of June, 1982, the executive committee
and many friends met together in Lafayette Park, across the
street from the White House, for a living witness. This time
the banner simply read: **NATIONAL CHRISTIAN
LEADERSHIP CONFERENCE FOR ISRAEL.** Isaac Rottenberg, NCLCI's Executive Director (operates the New
York office) had wisely rented a powerful sound truck. Four
large columns of speakers were set up. Later people told us
they could hear us almost a mile away. John Philip Lunati, an
outstanding musician, had flown in from Fort Myers, Florida.
At noon his powerful voice projected over the area in a

In Lafayette Park, June 15, 1982. NCLCI.

45

fifteen-minute concert. Soon the park was filled with tourists and government staff workers who were on their noon break. The meeting continued with prayer and speeches by various members of NCLCI. The speakers represented a wide spectrum of church affiliations: fundamentalists, Protestants, Catholics, old-line denominationalists, Pentecostals—people from all disciplines of the Christian faith.

During the final session of the NCLCI executive committee meeting the following statement was drafted as an expression of the whole group:

Draft statement adopted by the participants in the June 14-15, 1982, Strategy Sessions in Washington, D.C. We would welcome any comments you may wish to make.

The National Christian Leadership Conference for Israel is a coalition of Christian groups united for one single purpose: support for
• the security of the State of Israel
• the integrity of Jerusalem
• the survival of the people of Israel.
N.C.L.C.I. is an umbrella group composed of people with diverse racial, ethnic, political and doctrinal backgrounds. Member groups disagree with each other in many respects but they agree to work together in support of Israel.

The following telegram was sent to:
The National Association of Evangelicals
The National Council of Churches
The Roman Catholic Bishops
The Southern Baptist Convention
The leaders of five Black denominations

MEMBERS OF THE NATIONAL CHRISTIAN LEADERSHIP CONFERENCE FOR ISRAEL ARE CONVENED IN WASHINGTON, D.C., AT A HISTORIC TIME. WHILE DEPLORING WAR, WE

UNDERSTAND ISRAEL'S NEED TO PROTECT ITS PEOPLE FROM TERRORISM. AS A RESULT OF ISRAEL'S RIDDING LEBANON OF TERRORIST CENTERS, THE STABILITY OF THE REGION IS GREATLY ENHANCED.

WE URGE PROTESTANT AND CATHOLIC LEADERS TO ENCOURAGE OUR GOVERNMENT'S SUPPORT IN RESTORING SOVEREIGNTY TO THE GOVERNMENT OF LEBANON AND IN STRENGTH-ENING ISRAEL'S SECURITY. WE ASK ALL CHRISTIANS TO OFFER THEIR PRAYERS AND RESOURCES IN AIDING THE PEOPLE OF ISRAEL AND LEBANON.

—Executive Committee, NCLCI

Later I went to the offices of Morton Blackwell, special advisor to President Reagan, in the executive offices of the White House. There, with Bill Milhorn (member of NCLCI executive committee) we presented our point of view and objectives.

As the weeks rolled by and the crisis in Lebanon continued we observed the one-sided, unfair treatment the Israelis were receiving in the American press.

AN AD IN THE NEW YORK TIMES

Isaac Rottenberg called me to discuss the possibility of putting an advertisement in the *Washington Post* or the *New York Times*. After consulting with many of our people this was decided upon as a necessary course of action. Here is the text of that advertisement, placed in the *New York Times*, at a cost of over $15,000.

Christians in Solidarity With Israel

We speak as Christians who share a common concern for Israel notwithstanding many theological and political differences. Our solidarity with the Jewish people and the State of Israel is part of a commitment to peace and justice for all people in the Middle East.

47

We believe that it is the basic right and duty of every government to ensure the safety and security of its citizens. Hence we hold that the Israeli action against the heavily-armed PLO and Syrian forces in Lebanon was a justified response of a sovereign state to repeated provocations and attacks against Israel's civilian population in the Galilee.

Defaming the Jewish People We protest the widespread use of references to Hitler, genocide and the Holocaust in reports on the events in Lebanon. We believe that resort to such language has its source in a well-orchestrated campaign by those who not only oppose Israeli policies but seek to defame the Jewish people as a whole.

While we as Christians deeply lament all victims of this military action, and particularly the loss of life among civilians, we also note the growing number of independent reports from the scene confirming Israeli claims that the original casualty figures were highly exaggerated. We are deeply troubled that this technique of the "big lie" had such a strong impact on media coverage of the Lebanon situation.

An Opportunity for Lebanon We are encouraged by the voices coming from the Lebanese people themselves, telling the world about the true nature of the PLO and Syrian presence and about their own aspirations for a new Lebanon. We hope and pray that the Lebanese people will grasp the historic opportunity to reestablish a strong government with representation from all the people and serving the welfare of all the people.

We urge our own government to continue to work in close cooperation with Israel, our most dependable ally in the Middle East. Free of the PLO presence in Lebanon, our government can help explore the possibilities of reconstituting an independent and sovereign Lebanon as well as new opportunities that now exist for negotiations with Arab states and Palestinian Arabs for a durable peace in the Middle East.

Dr. Jimmy Allen
Pres., Southern Baptist
  Radio and Television
  Commission
Fort Worth, TX

Beverly Asbury
Vanderbilt University
Nashville, TN

Rev. Karl H. Baehr
United Church of
  Christ Minister
NYC

Rev. Clarence Balmer
Evangelical Free Church
St. Louis Park, MN

Rev. John C. Barbour
Exec. Dir., NCCJ
Jacksonville, FL

Mr. William Barnes
Anoka, MN

Mrs. Mary Rose Black
California Christian Committee
  for Israel
Berkeley, CA

Dr. Charles E. Blair
Calvary Temple
Denver, CO

Robert and Lois Blewett
Interfaith Seminars
Minneapolis, MN

Mr. David Blewett
Burnsville, MN

Mr. Ray Block
Iowans for Israel
Webster City, IA

Dr. Robert Boyd
Luther Seminary
St. Paul, MN

Rev. Bruce Bramlett
St. Mark's Episcopal Church
Teaneck, NJ

Rev. Ralph Brosrom
Dir., Midwest Christians
  for Israel
Bloomington, MN

Rev. Robert Bullock
New England Committee
  for Israel
Sharon, MA

Dr. Israel Carmona
Santa Ana, CA

Nancy Gabriela Carroll
NCLCI Exec. Committee
Winnetka, IL

John E. Chambers
Christian Friends of Israel
Topeka, KS

Rev. Rodger Claxton
St. John Lutheran Church
Annandale, MN

Dr. Rufus Cornelsen
Chmn., National Institute
  on the Holocaust
Philadelphia, PA

Herb Craft
Houston Area Chmn.,
  Christians for Israel
Houston, TX

John D. Craig,
Board of Dir.
  Christian Jewish Committee
  Concerned for Israel
Houston, TX

Dr. Archie Crouch
Americans Concerned for
  Israel and the Middle East
Englewood, NJ

Carla Cruzan
Minneapolis, MN

Dr. Philip Culbertson
Christ Episcopal Church
Oberlin, OH

Mr. and Mrs. Harold Dart
Christians for Israel
Bellingham, WA

Mr. Frederick J. Dean
Christians for Israel
Dallas, TX

Mr. James Doherty
Youth Institute for Peace
  in the Middle East
Los Angeles, CA

Rev. Wm. Ebling
"Committee of 50"
Bellflower, CA

Profs. Roy and Alice Eckardt
Lehigh University
Bethlehem, PA

Frank Eiklor
Shalom Fellowship
Keene, NH

Rev. Robert A. Everett
Emanuel United Church of Christ
Irvington, NJ

Rev. Jerry Falwell
Lynchburg, VA

Dr. James Farr
Asbury United Methodist Church
Orange Park, FL

Rev. Edward H. Flannery
Our Lady of Providence Seminary
Warwick, RI

Dr. Wendell Frerichs
Luther-Northwestern Seminary
St. Paul, MN

Rev. Peter Gardner
Salvation Army
Minneapolis, MN

Rev. Jess Gibson
Cornerstone Word Church
Springfield, MO

Sister Ann Gillen
Exec. Dir., National Religious
  Task Force on Soviet Jewry
Chicago, IL

Matthew R. Giuffrida
Dir., Parish Witness Program
American Baptist Churches–USA
Valley Forge, PA

Pastor John C. Hagee
"A Night to Honor Israel"
San Antonio, TX

Dr. Wm. and Rev. Linda Harter
Presbyterian Church
   of Falling Spring
Chambersburg, PA

Patrick W. Henning
Exec. Dir., Catholic Labor
   Instit. of So. California
Los Angeles, CA

Rev. Robert Hooley
Faith Bible Chapel
Denver, CO

Rev. H. Jacoba Hurst
St. Anne Episcopal Church
Tifton, GA

Dr. David Hyatt
Pres., NCCJ and ICCJ
NYC

Dr. John F.X. Irving
Former Law School Dean
Seton Hall University
Basking Ridge, NJ

Jim Jackson
U.S. Christian Embassy, Israel
Official Affiliate,
   Int. Christian Embassy, Jerusalem
Montreat, NC

Rev. Arthur Jones
St. Mark's AME Church
East Orange, NJ

Rev. Elmer A. Josephson
Bible Light International
Hillsboro, KS

Dr. Joe M. King
Furman University
Greenville, SC

Prof. Eugene and Lois Kreider
Luther-Northwestern Seminary
St. Columba School
St. Paul, MN

Douglas Krieger
TAV Evangelical Ministries
Sacramento, CA

Rev. Robert Kyte
United Church of Christ
Lenox, MA

Mrs. Elva Lanowick
Christian-Israel Friendship League
Paradise, CA

Howard Leighton-Floyd
Support Israel Christian Zionist Assoc.
Anderson, MO

Yvonne Lewerke
Iowa Christian Friends of Israel
Clearlake, IA

Dr. David A. Lewis
Christians United for Israel
Springfield, MO

Mrs. Walter Clay Lowdermilk
Honorary Chmn., California Christian
   Comm. for Israel
Berkeley, CA

Dr. Richard Lux
Sacred Heart School of Theology
Milwaukee, WI

Rev. James Lyons
Ecumenical Institute for
   Jewish-Christian Studies
Southfield, MI

Rev. Dan L. Martin
Congregational Church
Silverlake, MN

Sister Mary of Carmel
Hinesburg, VT

Edward E. McAteer
The Religious Roundtable
Arlington, VA

William Millhorn
Washington, DC

Rev. Jerry A. Moore, Jr.
Nineteenth Street Baptist Church
Washington, DC

Dr. F. Burton Nelson
North Park Theological Seminary
Chicago, IL

Dr. Franz Oerth
First Baptist Church
Needham, MA

Dr. Arnold T. Olson
Pres. Emeritus, Evangelical
   Free Church of America
Minneapolis, MN

Roderick Olson
Editor, Augsburg Publishing Co.
Minneapolis, MN

Rev. John T. Pawlikowski
Chicago Theological Union
Chicago, IL

Rev. John Peyton
Reconciliation Fellowship
Washington, DC

Dr. Samuel Pittman
Northwestern College
St. Paul, MN

Tom Poole
Carmel, ME

Dr. Robert Power-Ross
University of Minnesota
Minneapolis, MN

Dr. Sally Jo Power-Ross
Minneapolis, MN

The Rt. Rev. Quintin E. Primo, Jr.
Episcopal Diocese of Chicago
Chicago, IL

Rev. John Radano
Seton Hall University
East Orange, NJ

Dr. Otto Reimherr
Prof. Emeritus,
  Susquehanna University
Selingrove, PA

Sister Carol Rittner
Mercy College
Detroit, MI

Edmund W. Robb, Jr.
Chmn., Instit. on Religion
  and Democracy
Dallas, TX

Rev. Jerry Rose
Pres., Christian Communications
  of Chicagoland, Inc.
Chicago, IL

Paul O. Sand
Author/Lecturer
St. Paul, MN

Matthew Schwartz
Intercessors for Israel
Kansas City, MO

Hon. Albert J. Smith
Mayor, Skokie, IL

Rev. Carl R. Smith
Synod of Lincoln Trails
United Presbyterian Church
Indianapolis, IN

Rev. Thomas Stewart
Pres., American Friends
  of Nes Ammim
Buffalo, NY

Rev. Bruce Stuart
Augsburg College
Minneapolis, MN

Rev. Dr. Hilton Sutton
Mission to America
Humble, TX

Sister Rose Thering
Vice-Pres., America-Israel
  Friendship League
Seton Hall University
East Orange, NJ

Dr. John Townsend
Episcoal Divinity School
Cambridge, MA

Mary Ann Travers
Chicago Regional Office, NCCJ
Chicago, IL

Sister Margaret Ellen Traxler
Dir., Institute of Women Today
Chicago, IL

Dr. Paul Van Buren
Temple University
Philadelphia, PA

Dr. Carl Hermann Voss
Ecumenical Scholar in
  Residence, NCCJ
Jacksonville, FL

Clarence Wagner, Jr.
Bridges for Peace
Tulsa, OK

Sister Ann Patrick Ware
Vice-Pres., National Coalition
  of American Nuns
NYC

Rev. James T. Wheless
Consulate Dir., U.S. Christian
  Embassy, Israel
Houston, TX

Dr. Clark Williamson
Christian Theological Seminary
Indianapolis, IN

Dr. Robert and Elaine Willis
Hamline University
St. Paul, MN

Prof. Marvin Wilson
Gordon College
Wenham, MA

Dr. Charles J. Wissink
New Brunswick Theological Seminary
New Brunswick, NJ

Charles Woehrle
St. Paul, MN

Dr. Gerritt ten Zythoff
Chmn., Dept. of Religious Studies
Southwest Missouri State University
Springfield, MO

Organizations listed for identification purposes only.
This advertisement has been coordinated by the
**NATIONAL CHRISTIAN LEADERSHIP CONFERENCE
FOR ISRAEL**
and is sponsored by the above signatories. Please address
inquiries and tax-deductible contributions to defray the cost
of this ad to:
NCLCI, 134 East 39th Street, New York, NY 10016
(212) 679-4822
Dr. David A. Lewis, President
Dr. Franklin H. Littell, President Emeritus
Rev. Isaac C. Rottenberg, Executive Director

Along with the usual hate mail there came a flood of positive response to the advertisement. Many people all over the country asked permission to buy space in their local papers to reprint the ad. It has appeared in many outstanding newspapers from coast to coast. Some of the local sponsors proudly added their names to the list of signers.

The Israeli Embassy in Washington called Isaac to express appreciation for the *New York Times* advertisement. During the course of the conversation it was suggested that it would be profitable for the friends of NCLCI to put together a group to go to Lebanon and observe the actual condition there, to talk to the Lebanese people and find out how they viewed the entrance of Israel's defense forces into their country. Isaac learned that Cal Thomas, one of Jerry Falwell's people, was working on a similar project. They began to work together and in the end result each of them enlisted twenty-eight people for the fact-finding mission. The fifty-six participants were from diverse religious communities. Theologically far apart, they had one point of agreement, and that was that Israel has a right to a continued and secure existence in the Middle East.

David Lewis; Morton Blackwell, adviser to Reagan; Mrs. Ramona Lewis

The group left New York on August 9 and returned on the 13th. For some it was their first time in the Middle East. It was my thirtieth trip over. I had been in Lebanon in the spring of 1975 when the civil war broke out. We had to get out of Beirut on the first available flight, which took us to Amman, Jordan. This was my first time back to Lebanon since 1975, although I stood at the border of Southern Lebanon and met with various Lebanese such as Major Saad Hadaad and Mr. Francis Rizk each time I visited Israel in the intervening period.

We will share some of the content of the Israeli briefings, the session with Major Hadaad in Sidon, conversations with the Lebanese people and much more. You are in for a revelation you will never get from the television and newspaper reporting in the USA, although some journalists are now beginning to get their eyes opened and are beginning to change their positions.

PLO AND PALESTINIANS

It must be understood that when we speak of the PLO (terrorists) we are not talking about the Palestinian people. The difference we make between the two is both apparent and will be elaborated upon in this book.

6

DAMOR

Damor is the most totally devastated place I have ever seen. After spending some time in that miserable, abandoned Lebanese town I concluded that there was hardly a building that had not suffered major damage. Although the villagers had long since fled, there were Israeli soldiers everywhere, constantly patrolling the area.

If the American press were my only source of information I would have cried, "What monsters are these Israelis who so wantonly destroy the homes and businesses of almost 20,000 Lebanese Christians?" Some Western media had printed pictures of Damor, stating that the Israelis had smashed the town in their onslaught into Lebanon.

A bit of careful research, however, made me aware of an altogether different story behind the blatant lies of dissembling reporters.

The tragic story of Damor has been pieced together through reading of eyewitness accounts, our interviews with missionaries who were in Lebanon when it happened, from documents furnished to us by the Israelis, and finally from the Lebanese people themselves.

This Christian town of about 20,000 inhabitants was attacked and destroyed by the PLO in 1976. I have heard estimates that from 6,000 to 10,000 inhabitants were killed—while the rest of the population fled in terror. I talked to a missionary who was in Lebanon during the early part of the civil war (began in the spring of 1975). I told him how I had found the Lebanese people speaking of the Israelis as liberators, and asked why, in his opinion, the press had not spoken more of this aspect of the current situation. His reply was couched in almost bitter terms:

"The American press is not geared to honesty. Our press does not even have a concept of honesty. If they did they could not have taken and shown old pictures of devastation that took place years ago and make it appear as though it was something current."

I said, "Like at Damor; I know they did that. They showed pictures of Damor and indicated that it was Israeli-inflicted damage, but that was caused by the PLO."

My friend replied, "It certainly was. I was there in 1976 just after the PLO destroyed Damor. Our Bible School was taken over by the Christians of Damor, and they moved into

Inside the church. Part of it used as a garage for mechanical repairs, the altar for target practice.

55

the Bible School to live because they had no place else to live. Another missionary and I had some first-hand encounters with people who escaped the village of Damor. I used to go there regularly."

I asked, "Tell me, how was Damor destroyed, what actually happened there?"

"The PLO wanted it. They just went in and killed about everybody that was there."

When asked about the estimate that about 6,000 had been killed in Damor he said, "At least that many. They butchered people and dumped their bodies in the middle of the town and set them on fire, to add to the humiliation of the conquest of the Christian people there. Then the rest of the people fled in terror. The Christians (from elsewhere) flew in with helicopters to get them out. They fled by sea, they fled any way they could. The old people and the children who lagged behind were butchered by the PLO."

In all fairness we must say that not all the media has been dishonest. In fact, many reporters are changing their minds about the situation in the Mideast, once they themselves are exposed to the true facts. We will elaborate more on this in a later chapter.

Concerning Damor, on June 21, 1982 David K. Shipler reported in the *New York Times.*

For Christian Villagers, Happiness Amid Rubble
DAMOR, Lebanon, June 19—Abdullah Shaya, a 54-year-old gardener with a round, tanned face, found his house amid the rubble of Damor today. Unlike most of the stone and concrete buildings in the hillside village, it was intact, somehow spared the flying shrapnel from the bombs and shells that had ravaged the town and filled the streets with dust and chunks of rock.

"For seven years I have not passed this doorstep," he said as he stood outside, savoring the moment. Then he strode into his small dwelling and began to look around.

Damor, just south of Beirut, was a Christian village until January 1976, when its population fled an assault by Palestinian and leftist forces fighting in the Lebanese civil war. For nearly seven years, until the Israeli Army attacked and captured it last week, the town was inaccessible to its own people; the Palestine Liberation Organization made it a stronghold, using the churches as firing ranges and armories.

A huge new church, left unfinished by the fleeing Maronite Christians in 1976, is covered with spray-painted Palestinian nationalist slogans and plastered with posters of Al Fatah, the main PLO arm, and other Palestinian factions.

On an inside wall where the altar was to have stood, two bull's eyes can be seen in faded paint, the stone in and around them roughened by bullet holes. Above them, where a cross would have hung, a triangular PLO symbol is painted in the Palestinian nationalist colors of red, green, black and white, framing a silhouette of a rifle and a hammer. High in the belfry, a concrete cross has obviously been used as a target over the years, for it is chipped and gouged in a thousand places.

Damor—a Christian town destroyed by the PLO in 1976. Thousands of Christians were slaughtered.

A mortar on wheels stands inside the church's big doors, along with a jeep and a military truck. Posters on the walls show the Star of David being shattered by a wedge drawn in the Palestinian colors. In a once-elegant old church next door, crates of ammunition and drums of fuel are stored.

One corner of the old building was hit by a bomb or an artillery shell during the Israeli attack, and its heavy stone blocks tumbled into a narrow street. But the new church was carefully and successfully avoided; a building just 30 feet away lies in complete ruins, evidently hit by an aerial strike that left the church unscathed.

Christians Tentatively Returning

After Israeli troops took Damor and drove the Palestinians out, Prime Minister Menachem Begin announced that the Christians, whom Israel has supported for several years, would be allowed to return and rebuild. And now the first few former residents have tentatively come to pick through the rubble and see what remains.

Nothing of Mr. Shaya's own things were left. The couches and chair askew in the living room, the dirty pots and pans, the women's makeup on a corner table, the plastic flowers, the beds with their charred mattresses and sheets as if a small fire had raged—these belonged to the Palestinian invaders, not to his family.

The floor was littered with fragments of glass. A large poster of Yasir Arafat, the PLO leader, hung on the living room wall. Mr. Shaya, in tears and anger, grabbed it and tore it down, tearing it into shreds and throwing it onto the floor. A desk blotter, with a portrait of some leader he did not recognize, he could not tear, and so he bent it and sailed it out the door across a wall and out of sight.

"My family had lived here for 200 years, since the beginning of Damor," he said. "We worked in the orchards, grew lemons."

That pleasant, pastoral life ended in 1976. Since then, he said, "we have all been dead. If somebody doesn't have a home and doesn't have a village, what does he have to live for? Now we have started to live. My age is one hour old."

"What More Can I Say?"

Mr. Shaya, who fled the Palestinians by sea to the northern port of Junieh and spent the intervening years living in a Christian suburb of Beirut, spoke in a loud voice that rang through the streets of the deserted town. He turned to an Israeli soldier. "What more can I say than thank you that you brought us back to our place," he said. "And God help you to get back to your place."

Walid Azzi, 27 years old, talked in similar images of death and life. "Outside Damor I feel myself like a dead man," he said. "But coming back here I am very happy."

What he found was not at all joyous, for his house was gone. "It is totally destroyed," he said. "Nothing remains, absolutely nothing. But we are happy anyway.

The PLO desecrated this church.

We are returning to our village, our land. I was very happy. I took some earth and I made it so." To demonstrate, he grinned broadly, picked up some dust and sprinkled it on his head.

"I am very happy," he said. "I can't explain it. Just because our land is back to us."

And what of the future? "The Israelis are my friends," Mr. Azzi said, "and I hope they stay for some time with us. Our liberty is not sure. But maybe if the big countries make something for us, we will be sure."

Church in Damor—desecrated by PLO terrorists.

Mr. Shaya saw it in simpler terms. "God will give all of us more years," he said, "and we will all come back and live in this village."

Just after my return from Lebanon I was visiting in the home of a friend on Long Island. His mother is a Roman Catholic and hearing our conversation pointed out a letter to the editor in a locally published religious tabloid, *THE LONG ISLAND CATHOLIC*. In the August 5, 1982 edition a Mr. S. G. wrote:

Christians' Plight

Editor: It is more in sorrow than anger that I raise a question you no doubt have been asked before. How is it that during the Lebanese civil war, when Christians were killed and wounded in the tens of thousands by the PLO and Syrians, not a single outcry came from the media, the Church or the left liberal PLO claque about the plight of the Christians?

Now that Israel has stormed its tormentor and would-be destroyer in his lair, a massive, seemingly orchestrated outcry responds to the wildly exaggerated assertions about the number of homeless, killed and wounded. Arafat's brother slipped the number of 600,000 homeless to the Lebanese Red Crescent Society, about 100,000 more people than in the entire population involved. This lie and also the number of killed and wounded was disseminated with great indignation throughout the world. The only exception was the Lebanese Christian populace who knew better, and who greeted the Israelis as liberators from the PLO. Evans and Novak, no champions of Israel, testified to this in their newspaper column. Is there an answer, or is it simply part of an ongoing attempt to delegitimate Israel and a continuation of the ancient practice of anti-Semitism?

Mr. S. G.
New York

61

7

MEETING WITH MAJOR SAAD HADDAD IN 1980

I met with Major Haddad in Mettulah, Israel, at the Arazim Hotel in the fall of 1980. I had been asked by an American author to accompany him to Israel and introduce him to leaders who could give him interviews upon which he could base a new book. After probing his intentions, I was satisfied that his approach was all right, so I went with him. I introduced this man to Prime Minister Begin, Dr. Reuben Hecht, Professor Benjamin Netanayahu, Lucian Harris, Moshe Yeager, leaders in the Christian community of Israel. And also introduced him to the McWhirters and a host of others. Finally we went to see Major Haddad.

Haddad is the commander of the Southern Lebanese Christian Militias. Over half of his soldiers are, however, Moslems, not Christians. Haddad himself is a devout Christian man. From my conversation with him I was satisfied that he is a born-again believer. The George Otis interviews with Major Haddad bear this out. Here is part of the interview we conducted with Haddad.

After I had given Haddad a long introduction of our purposes in the interview I posed the question: "We have heard of Israeli terrorists from our news media and from the State Department as well as PLO terrorists activity. They say that Israel is mounting terrorist operations against Lebanon. Could you comment on this?"

HADDAD: "I would like for them to come and visit all Lebanon, and especially the south. They will know that the PLO terrorists are ruling the area. They are making the rules. They are making the government. They are making their own laws. So the south became a big base of terrorists."

LEWIS: "You mean PLO terrorists?"

HADDAD: "I mean the PLO. There is no room for Lebanese self-rule there any more. If we are fighting here it is just against the terrorists. They are shooting us in our villages and we have to answer. No one seems to care how much we are suffering. We are surrounded on all sides. We have only one way open for us. It is to the south (Israel). They (PLO) threaten to exterminate us. Who are the PLO? They are a foreign organization, some of them Palestinian people, some from communist countries. There are Cubans, Italians, Czechoslovakians, in fact, from most all the communist countries."

Lewis and Haddad meeting in 1980 at Mettulah, Israel

LEWIS: "Netanayahu said that terrorism is international. All inter-related, Marxist in nature."

HADDAD: "Also from all the fanatic Islamic countries. You can find PLO from Libya, Iran, Egypt (those against Sadat), all the Arab countries. These are the PLO we are facing. This is the PLO your State Department is giving moral support to. Those are the people they are trying to protect. They are destroying all human principle. The terrorists are frightening the Arab countries. Because the oil rich countries are afraid of the PLO they are giving them money, as much as they want, as long as they will keep away from their country.

"The PLO are criminals. They have burned our whole country that used to be a paradise. Now there is no more Lebanon. They committed the biggest crime in history. They killed our whole country."

LEWIS: "The PLO say they want to destroy Israel and establish a Palestinian state. Do you think their aims are bigger than this?"

HADDAD: "They consider themselves a revolution for the whole Middle East. They want to change all the regimes in the Middle East. They want to make it communist. And it is always in their program to destroy and finish with Israel.

"Why do they always attack Israel from the south of Lebanon? Why not work from Syria, why not from Jordan? The Syrians won't allow them any military uniform in Syria. Jordan struck at them in September 1970, the 'Black September' you know, and no one opened his mouth. Only in Lebanon they are holy and sacred. Why? Because Lebanon is a weak country. Because too many want all the Christians in Lebanon to disappear. Because Lebanon is the only Mideast country ruled by a Christian president."

LEWIS: "Most of the Christians in Lebanon are Catholic. Has the Pope spoken out for you at all? Has he said anything to help you?"

HADDAD: "No, unfortunately, no, until now he didn't."

LEWIS: "Is he afraid?"

HADDAD: "He thinks that if he makes such a declaration that the Christians in the rest of the Arab world will suffer. But, from my point of view, even with that he should say to all the Christian world: 'Wake up! Help your brothers in Lebanon who are being exterminated.' Anyhow, if the Christians in Lebanon are exterminated the other Christians in the Middle East will also be exterminated. The major community of Christians is in Lebanon, so that is security for all the other Christians in the Arab countries. If this community will be finished, they will finish with the others and it will be too late."

LEWIS: "The news said that the Pope met with a representative of Arafat, the leader of the PLO. It was a friendly meeting."

HADDAD: "I am ashamed to hear such news . . . the Pope receiving this criminal in the Vatican. It is a shame. They should visit our towns and see what the PLO makes of our churches. They made a toilet of the church in one village. If the PLO gets Jerusalem they will do the same with the Christian holy places there. They have changed many churches to mosques."

LEWIS: "What role is the UN playing here? What is the United Nations doing in Lebanon?"

HADDAD: "They are doing nothing. They are here only because the UN Security Council decided they should be here. They are just a picture. They can't do much more. Sometimes they are offering help and cover to the PLO. The UN is not ready to fight them so they accept them. Last night the PLO fired some katyusha rockets from inside a UN position into our villages. Some of the PLO circulate with official UN documents and identification as liaison officers. They use this authority against us."

LEWIS: "Is it true that the Israeli's help has been welcomed by the Lebanese Christians?"

HADDAD: "That is the only country which cared for us. Without Israel we would have been exterminated a long time ago. In fact, some Christian villages have been exterminated, like Damor and others. In Damor they even slaughtered the children. We are not ready to accept that. I ask you to send a committee to Damor. Make an inquiry of what happened there. You can see why we are so thankful for Israel. The country which is supposed to be our enemy is supporting us. And our friends are leaving us. We are poor people. We have no oil. We have nothing to sell to them. Only Israel has helped us."

LEWIS: "Is is true that the Moslems in the area cooperate with you?"

HADDAD: "About 60 percent of the population is Moslem in this area. They are cooperating with us. There is no difference of level of life. We are the same, sharing the same life, facing the same enemy. Why? Because they understand that its a question of survival. They know they are not coming (PLO) to help the Muslims. They are coming to make their own revolution and to take the land for themselves. They are enslaving the local people."

LEWIS: "Your homes can suffer attack at any time then?"

HADDAD: "Sure, I told you last night they shot rockets against us. About five kilometers (three miles) from here is one of their main strongholds, Castle Beaufort, which was once a Christian Crusader stronghold, now it is being used to fight against the Christians.

"I urge all Americans to come and see Lebanon for themselves. See how we are living. We love the American people."

LEWIS: "Most of the people in America would be in sympathy with you if they knew the facts."

HADDAD: "I am thankful for your good will. I have not lost hope with the American people, because I know they have a good heart. We love them. We are the real friends of America, not the PLO or the Syrians. You cannot count on them. You can count on us, we won't change."

8

SIDON

After journeying through Tyre and Damor we arrived in Sidon. Our group of 56 journalists, pastors and teachers from various religious communities walked the streets talking to shoppers, shop keepers, local residents. I talked to well over 100 people, singly and to small groups. It was common to find people who had a fair knowledge of English, so communication was not a major problem.

I asked each person I talked to how they felt about the presence of Israeli soldiers in their country. Was the situation now better or worse than it had been before? Without exception every person I talked to said the same thing: "The situation is far better." Many said they welcomed the Israelis as liberators.

Horror stories of the PLO occupation were told. Rape of women of all ages was common. Even small girls were raped and often killed to eliminate evidence. PLO terrorists would enter the homes of the Lebanese and take over. Sometimes the family would be allowed to remain in one room. More often than not they were simply kicked out completely. Young boys were conscripted into the terrorist forces along with their older brothers. I heard accounts of boys as young as twelve years being forced to serve in the PLO. We heard vivid tales of unusual brutality. We were told that in one PLO-controlled hospital when they ran out of blood for transfusions living persons were fastened to the wall and drained of their blood for wounded PLO members. If I understand it, the transfusions were made direct from the victim to the patient. The victimized Lebanese would be so misused until his blood supply was so low he simply died.

REBUILDING LEBANON

The Lebanese are an industrious and aggressive people. Although the towns are damaged (not destroyed) rebuilding was already going on. Everywhere heavy cranes and building equipment was in operation. Bricklayers were at work. Bulldozers were clearing away the rubble to make way for new construction.

The shops were open for business and a brisk trade was taking place. Traffic was so heavy at times that we were actually caught in traffic jams.

MEETING WITH MAJOR SAAD HADDAD

Once again it was a privilege to meet with Major Haddad. The group went to his military headquarters for a briefing. Here are a few of his comments.

"We have been living in a very bad situation for the last seven years. We lost hope. The people of Beirut lost hope that they could ever again breathe freely, that they could walk in the street freely with their head raised. Then a miracle happened. Israel intervened. Not only to assure the safety of the Galilee, but also to liberate Lebanon and to help the Lebanese people to recuperate. The proof of that miracle is that we are here together. Without Israeli intervention it was impossible to save Lebanon. Lebanon was in danger of disappearing. . . .

"Lebanon was the biggest base for international terrorism. This action of Israel was also to fight international terrorism, and to save the free world from international terror. We are so thankful for the action of Israel. We are calling it the liberation of Lebanon. We hope that ALL of Lebanon will be liberated. We hope that the terrorists and the Syrians will withdraw from Lebanon. We are sure that then Israel will withdraw and grant full authority for the Lebanese to rule their own country.

Sidon: We found most of the city not damaged.

Sidon: Fortunately we had an Israeli army officer with us!

Sidon: Israeli soldier buys a pair of shoes.

Damaged buildings in Sidon.

Moslem mosque in Sidon

In Sidon life comes back to normal. A family going to the beach.

"We are not going to abandon our relation with Israel. On the contrary, we insist that our relation with Israel will be based on the purpose to serve for peace in the Middle East and all the world. We want to make a peace agreement with Israel. We are not going to accept something else, or any pressure that would prevent this peace agreement. We were abandoned by all the rest of the world. Only Israel sacrificed for us and helped us. This experience of the cooperation— between Christians and Jews—it is something rare, it is something new, but it is successful .... We as Christians believe that our roots are coming from the Jewish religion."

QUESTION: "How much religion is involved in the civil war? Was it really true religious conviction or just political labels?"

HADDAD: "From here to the Israeli border there are about 700,000 people of all religions. Until now, since the IDF (Israel Defense Forces) operation we have not had any incident between the Christians and the Muslims. That proves it was not a religious war. All of that was propaganda made by the terrorists and the Syrians to cover their action in Lebanon and to deceive the world about what was going on in Lebanon."

EXTENSIVE PLO INSTALLATIONS

The military spokesman travelling with us and the officer giving another briefing in Sidon informed us that there were enough arms to furnish an army of a half million men. It was stated that documents were found indicating that a major military action was set for August 4, 1982. This PLO fronted action would be to totally take over Lebanon, to invade Israel, and ultimately to control the entire Middle East. The spokesman who was with us for a while, on the bus, began commenting on the extensive underground installations. He wondered at the massive amounts of concrete and steel that had been used to build these subterranean strongholds. He said that it took 10,000 pounds of explosives to destroy some of the bunkers. Only a few of the underground warrens were destroyed, however.

9

A VOICE FROM LEBANON

**Lebanese Leader Calls Israeli Action
In Lebanon "Long Overdue"**
Dory Chamoun, son of former President Camille
Chamoun of Lebanon, made the following statement at a
news conference held at the Pierre Hotel in New York on 22
June 1982:

*For most of us Lebanese, the Israeli invasion has been
long overdue. Having failed politically and diplomatically to
rid Lebanon of Syrian and Palestinian occupation, we became
more and more convinced that Lebanon could only be freed by
military action.*

*The fact that we Lebanese did not possess the
necessary military clout meant that we were either doomed to
remain occupied for a long period of time, or that someone
else had to assume the role.*

*Because of the PLO's behavior in Lebanon and their
attacks on Israel, we knew that there would come a time when
Israel would have to perform that surgical operation which
we had been unable to accomplish. We had warned Palestinian and Arab leaders time and again, as far back as 1968,
that PLO behavior in Lebanon is unacceptable and was going
to bring about such action on the part of Israel—but to no
avail. The reason we gave such warnings was not to safe-*

guard the PLO but to try and save Lebanon from war and destruction.

Our warnings also went to the Western world which was at one time prepared to see Lebanon disappear under the Palestinian and Syrian boot, not realizing that in so doing they were, in reality, making of Lebanon a gift to the Soviet Union. What more evidence is there to this than the Soviet reaction to the Israeli invasion of Lebanon when Moscow protested and declared very solemnly that such an invasion was against Russian interests in the area.

Frankly, what worries us most is not the invasion as such—those who have suffered seven years of war and destruction can endure a few more days. We are worried about the outcome—will this finally mean freedom, security and the end of a nightmare, or will United States pressure once again force a solution of compromise which will satisfy no one and just perpetuate the miseries of the inhabitants of that region?

Summary of the question-answer period following Chamoun's statement:

1. In answer to a question relating to the order of removal of foreign forces from Lebanon, Chamoun replied: "First the PLO, then the Syrians and finally Israel."

2. When questioned about the number of casualties, Chamoun answered that, according to their estimates, some 2,500-2,600 were killed and about 100,000 are homeless— although many of these are already returning to their homes.

3. Regarding his party's relations with Major Saad Haddad, Chamoun suggested that Haddad should continue to serve in his present position. He added that Haddad is working towards the same goal as his own party but, because of the situation in Lebanon, they have been forced to work separately.

4. Questioned whether his party had given the green light to Israel before the Israel Defense Forces went into action, Chamoun answered that the Israelis did not need any green light to act, and that they had not asked for one.

5. Asked if he knew in advance about the Israeli action, Chamoun replied: "Of course; after all, the Israelis had been

74

making their intentions known loudly and clearly for several months."

6. In the course of a number of his answers, Chamoun made a point of separating himself from Israel and to explain that he was not a "puppet" of the Israelis. For example, when asked about a particular statement of Defense Minister Sharon, he replied that Sharon speaks in Israel's name, while he speaks in the name of Lebanon.

Ramona Lewis at the Lebanon/Israel border.

10

BEIRUT

We came to the southern part of Beirut after our visit to the coastal cities to the south. This was before the agreement had been reached relative to removing the PLO from the city. The fighting was going on. The area we walked around in was the location of an Israeli command post. There was an observation station and several pieces of heavy artillary which fired intermittently. The first few rounds that went off startled a number of our people. It was evident from the damage shown on some of the buildings that firing was coming our way from time to time as well.

Amazingly enough, right here in this area south of the airport, rebuilding and construction was going on. The Lebanese are surely a determined people.

THE BIG BOMBARDMENT
Right after we left, the controversial 11-hour bombardment of Beirut was ordered by Israeli General Sharon. The next day I sat in the stormiest session in the history of the Israeli Knesset (parliament). Retired General Bar Lev rose to his feet, shouting at Begin who was speaking. He literally screamed with rage as he hurled insulting accusations against Begin. Begin shouted right back at him. General Sharon stood up, trembling with rage and entered

the verbal battle. Suddenly most of the Knesset members were on their feet shouting and arguing. A couple became physical and began pushing and shoving. Security guards literally dragged two members out of the room. Most of our group was out touring the Knesset building, but I was able to get myself and two others into the proceedings of the Knesset. After the Knesset speech, Begin left. We saw him out in the hall. He recognized me and called out my name. We chatted for a few moments, then he went down to give our entire group a briefing.

DAMAGED—NOT DESTROYED

We found Beirut to be a badly damaged city, but not a destroyed city (like Berlin at the close of WW 2). The Israelis expressed regret at the civilian casualties, but it must be remembered that the PLO always put its forces in civilian areas. This was the major cause of civilian casualties.

Reconstruction in war-torn Beirut. While fighting continued, we found a city damaged but not totally destroyed.

DISTORTIONS OF THE PRESS

The media greatly inflated the casualty figures. The press showed pictures of damage done by the PLO and the Syrians during the civil war that had been going on since 1975, and attributed the damage to the Israelis. The New York Times has printed an apology and clarification. They had used a picture of a baby, saying that the child was hurt in an Israeli bombing of a hospital. The article said that the baby had lost both its arms. With the apology was printed the original picture of the baby (in a blanket) and a current picture of the baby in its mother's arms. The child had not lost any limbs. It did have a broken arm.

PRESS BEGINS TO CHANGE

Some members of the press began to see that there was a defense of the Israeli action and position. Some began tentatively to bring this out. Others realized that if they ever wanted any credibility they would have to give a nod to the truth.

The Near East Report (August 13, 1982) reported on John Chancellor's change of attitude.

JOHN CHANCELLOR'S CHANGE

In the past week, television viewers were treated to a strange spectacle—the metamorphosis of NBC's commentator John Chancellor.

His evolution is instructive.

Chancellor had never analyzed Israel's actions. He reacted as if by reflex. When Israeli ground forces crossed the border with the declared objective of creating a security zone around the Galilee, Chancellor instantly came out swinging.

In his commentary on June 7, the day after Israeli forces went in, Chancellor condemned Israel for "trying to buy a few years of peace at a terrible human and political cost" while "making the American policy in the Middle East a shambles."

Chancellor seemed to have forgotten the PLO shelling of the northern Galilee and PLO attacks against Israeli citizens. His was a relentless drumbeat against

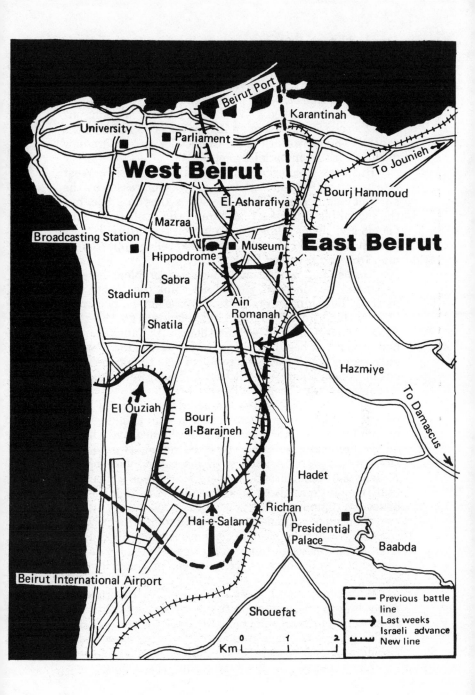

Km 0 1 2

Previous battle line
Last weeks Israeli advance
New line

79

Israel which continued in a commentary on the Falklands and Lebanon on June 12.

Chancellor went to the area and there his initial charges became more hysterical. Standing on a hill overlooking Beirut, while plumes of smoke rose from the city, Chancellor asked: "What in the world is going on? Israel's security problem on its border is 50 miles to the south." The answer, thought Chancellor, is "we are now dealing with an imperial Israel. . . . "

But then Chancellor left the hills overlooking West Beirut and entered East Beirut. He was impressed by the normalcy and calm. "There are still scores to settle, but the incredible thing we find here is the resiliency of the people and their willingness to bet on the future."

On August 6, a new John Chancellor appeared—a man who had reversed his position.

"Israel had a legitimate security problem here in Lebanon," he conceded. He did not think the danger was mortal, "but things were getting worse and no one knew how far the disintegration of Lebanon might go. With the PLO in charge here, it was as though Al Capone's mob had been given heavy artillery, so Israel decided that the only way it could solve the problem was to get the PLO out of Lebanon and see to it that Lebanon would become strong enough to keep the PLO out."

Chancellor charged that Israel always planned to go past the 40 km. limit but miscalculated in thinking that most of the civilian population would flee and that a quick diplomatic solution could be found, two concessions which were at odds with his earlier view of the Israelis as bloodthirsty murderers. He was conceding that Israelis do not want to kill civilians and that they do believe in diplomacy.

Chancellor's manner, too, was different. His previous comments had been pronouncements from on high, delivered with certitude and authority. But his Friday comments were more contemplative, preceded by the words, "I believe. . . . "

Why the change? It does not seem to be pressure. According to NBC, reaction to his earlier comments was running half pro and half con. (NBC took the unusual step of airing some of the letters angry viewers had written.) Nor did it appear to be pressure from network executives.

What seems to have wrought the change was

Chancellor's visit to the scene where he could see the area and its people for himself.

If this change is permanent, we may have a commentator of stature. We will be watching Chancellor closely in the future. Such an admission of a mistake and such an overwhelming change in the space of a week, shows there may be some hope for the media.

—David Silverberg

The Near East Report also had this to say:

WHAT THE MEDIA DID NOT DO

Questions which were not asked were as important as those which were.

There was little or no probing of how the Israeli operation might advance American interests, no exploration of the resulting new diplomatic opportunities, no investigation of the implications of this blow to Soviet ambitions.

Similarly, to date, little effort has been made to concentrate on the pattern of PLO delays, ruses, and other tricks to prevent their removal from Lebanon. Nor has much been said about the PLO's failure to honor its own written agreements—signed with other Arab countries—pledging not to introduce heavy arms in Lebanon or conduct armed operations from Lebanese soil. By omission in the media, the American public is ignorant of the fact that the PLO has a long history of broken promises and broken agreements.

New policy concepts came mainly in the form of Op-Ed pieces and editorials by foreign policy analysts—virtually never from reporters and correspondents actually covering the story. The mass of the press corps instead continued pursuing the faults of the operation, rather than the benefits.

By failing to raise these questions, the media all but eliminated the public's awareness of them. As a result, the Administration and public have been led to give undue emphasis to one set of policy options at the expense of those which might further the American national interest.

POINTS TO CONSIDER

For seven years, Israel tried through diplomatic means

to end PLO attacks from Lebanon. But no sovereign state can tolerate indefinitely shellings and raids from neighboring territory. International law specifically provides, in such a case, that the victim has the right of reprisal and intervention to end the threat.

Israel's actions will bring peace not only for the Israeli communities which were being subjected to repeated attack by the PLO, but also for the people of Lebanon who will at last be freed from the tyranny of armed guerrillas in their midst. Lebanon had been, before the PLO and Syrian invasions, an island of democracy in a sea of Arab tyrannies, and a state at peace with Israel. The PLO plunged the country into civil war and turned it into the world headquarters of terrorism. Israel has stopped the decline of Lebanon into anarchy, and created an opportunity to restore order and rebuild a democratic society.

The PLO and Syria are the Soviet Union's closest allies in the Middle East and sworn enemies of the United States. Israel has dealt a major setback to these instruments of the Soviet Union, reducing the influence of Moscow in the region and creating new opportunities for American diplomacy.

At the same time, Israel has weakened significantly the radical and rejectionist camp within the Arab world. It may now be possible for King Hussein to challenge the PLO's claim to be sole representative of the Palestinians and become involved in the Camp David negotiations. Egypt will regain a central position in the Arab world. Negotiations for peace will be given a boost if the Arab moderates seize this opportunity to break the stranglehold over diplomatic compromise that has been held by PLO assassins.

The PLO is the hub of the international terrorist network. It is permanently committed to the destruction of Israel and pretends to "compromise" only to achieve short-term tactical gains. It has a long history of violating written agreements, such as the Cairo (1969), Malkert (1973), and Shtaura (1977) agreements in which it promised the other Arabs it would not conduct armed operations from Lebanon. It does not negotiate in good faith. It must leave Beirut and

Lebanon altogether for there to be peace in that country.

While civilian casualties in any war are tragic, American understanding of Lebanon has been confused by the uncritical acceptance of wildly inflated casualty figures emanating from the PLO "Red Crescent," which is headed by Arafat's brother. Even the highest estimates of civilian casualties since June 6 put them at less than 10% the loss of civilian life which resulted from the preceding seven years of PLO and Syrian terror in Lebanon. Had the previous situation continued, many more Lebanese civilians would have fallen victim—probably without provoking much notice in the West. The civilian casualty issue has become a tool in the campaign to villify Israel, rather than a genuine human rights issue.

Prime Minister Begin with Arab leader Saad Haddad of Lebanon. Haddad has shown himself to be a friend of Israel. Mr. Begin's government has given aid to the Christian population of Lebanon. Begin hopes for a peace treaty with Lebanon.

Israel's action in Lebanon serves the strategic interests of the United States and will help promote a lasting peace in the region.

THE PLO PRESENCE IN BEIRUT

The PLO is a terrorist organization whose central aim is the liquidation of Israel. In pursuit of this aim, the organization has been operating, from its bases in Lebanon, both against Israel and against Jews abroad.

Israel is convinced that the only way to ensure that its citizens will henceforth be able to live securely and in peace is to remove the PLO from Lebanon. This has been accomplished in Southern Lebanon, where the PLO bases no longer exist; but parts of its forces and headquarters remain in West Beirut.

The headquarters of the PLO's various component groups have been set up in the western part of the Lebanese capital—in total disregard of the authority and sovereignty of the Lebanese government. For the past twelve years the city has served as the main center for PLO organizational activities of all kinds, including the planning of terrorist strikes and the training and activation of terrorists against Israel and other countries. In Beirut today there are between 5,000 and 6,000 terrorists, together with their leaders.

Beirut has also been the hub of the organization's intelligence, publication and propaganda apparatus. Its newspapers have been published there, and the broadcasts of its radio station, "The Voice of Palestine," have been beamed to the surrounding region from Beirut. The PLO news agency, "Wafa," has its offices in Beirut.

In Beirut was the center of international terror, with active links to virtually every known terrorist underground in the world. The city also housed the administrative, logistical and technical facilities connected with terrorist activity abroad; a travel agency, printing presses, facilities for forging passports, and workshops and storage places for arms, ammunition and explosive devices.

Like the rest of Southern Lebanon, the city of Beirut was turned into an enclave of piracy and lawlessness under PLO domination. So long as the Lebanese capital is not rid of these terrorist groups and their facilities, Lebanon will not be able to restore the lawful and effective rule of its government or exercise sovereignty there; nor will the welfare of its citizens—or the citizens of Israel—be assured. Israel is certain that all the nations of the enlightened world support the restoration of Lebanese sovereignty, the disarming of the PLO and the elimination of one of the main centers of world terrorism.

11

THE IMAGE OF THE ISRAELI SOLDIER

(A letter to Israel Defense Forces [IDF] soldiers from the
IDF's Chief Education Officer, 11 June 1982.)

*Now that the aims of Operation Peace for Galilee to guarantee
safety of our citizens in the north have been achieved, Israel has
initiated a cease-fire.*

*Israel has called upon Syria to adhere to the conditions of the
cease-fire in order to stabilize the situation in Lebanon.*

*The Israel Defense Forces (IDF) is now situated over
extensive areas of Lebanon; soldiers are coming into contact with a
large, diversified civilian population. This contact presents you with
a challenge—to behave in a humane, Jewish and IDF fashion.*

*The Chief Military Prosecutor has published binding
instructions to ensure such behaviour:*

* *It is absolutely forbidden to take spoils from any source
whatsoever. Anyone violating this order can expect a trial and a
maximum sentence of ten years in prison.*

* *Roadblocks have been placed on all exit roads from
Southern Lebanon; everyone leaving the area will be checked.*

* *The peaceful civilian population must not be harmed; in
particular, respect for women must not be violated.*

* *All IDF soldiers must refrain from harming sites of cultural
value, including archaeological sites, museums and the like.*

* *It is forbidden to harm the holy sites of any religion.*

Every war stirs up feelings of hatred, revenge and disrespect for enemy life and property. Despite these feelings, every one, as a human being, must observe those morals and principles on which the existence of human society is based.

This time, the IDF is fighting a cruel enemy, who systematically used terror against defenseless civilians.

The IDF must not act according to the standards accepted by our enemies; we must not allow feelings of revenge to guide our behaviour towards the civilian population in Lebanon. Our uniqueness, and our power, derive from our behaviour as decent human beings.

A deterioration of the rules of moral conduct in the IDF, which is a "people's army," will hurt you as a man and a citizen, and will have its effect on the moral level of Israeli society and on its quality of life.

The maintenance of the rules of fitting behaviour during your stay in Lebanon will also help Israel in its political and public opinion campaigns.

Part of the civilian population in Lebanon has shown itself ready to cooperate with Israel. One of the goals of Operation Peace for the Galilee was "the hope that a peace treaty will be signed with an independent Lebanon, its territorial integrity preserved." This is why the initial contact between IDF personnel and the citizens of Lebanon is so important. This contact is what will determine the character of future relations between two good neighbors.

Therefore, in your contacts with civilians you must show a proper, humane attitude, and take care to respect their dignity. In addition, you must help prevent acts of violence, robbery and looting among the Lebanese citizens themselves.

The eyes of the world are now on our region. Many journalists and foreign correspondents are now in the combat zone.

Acts of looting, or damage to property, holy places, cultural sites or natural or scenic areas will play into the hands of our enemies. You must see yourselves as having personal responsibility for the image of the IDF and of the State of Israel in the eyes of the citizens of Lebanon and of world public opinion.

The principles of morality are basic to the Jewish heritage. Even in wartime, it must be remembered that to his fellow man, a human being is a human being.

Israeli soldier in Lebanon

"And Joshua said unto Achan ... tell me now what thou hast done; hide it not from me. And Achan answered Joshua, and said, Indeed I have sinned against the Lord God of Israel, and thus and thus have I done: When I saw among the spoils a goodly Babylonian garment, and two hundred shekels of silver, and a wedge of gold of fifty shekels weight, then I coveted them, and took them; and, behold, they are hid in the earth in the midst of my tent, and the silver under it. So Joshua sent messengers, and they ran unto the tent; and, behold, it was hid in his tent, and the silver under it. And they took them out of the midst of the tent, and brought them unto Joshua, and unto all the children of Israel, and laid them out before the Lord. And Joshua, and all Israel with him, took Achan the son of Zerah, and the silver, and the garment, and the wedge of gold, and his sons, and his daughters, and his oxen, and his asses, and his sheep, and his tent, and all that he had, and they brought them unto the valley of Achor. And Joshua said, Why hast thou troubled us? The Lord shall trouble thee this day" (Joshua 7:19-25).

12

BACK TO JERUSALEM

After our time in Lebanon our group of fifty-six returned to Israel, to spend a night at the Diplomat Hotel, and on the following day to have briefings from Mr. Meridor (member of Begin's cabinet, Minister of Economic and Industrial Development), from Prime Minister Begin and from Former Prime Minister Rabin.

Meridor spoke of Israel's phenomenal success against the Russian planes and equipment, the taking out of the SAM missiles. He seemed to imply a supernatural intervention on Israel's behalf. He said, "It is difficult to explain, even for the non-believers. But then they have to start to believe as well. This war is changing the whole situation. And instead of calling in Mr. Begin and all his cabinet to the oval office in the White House and give every one a medal of merit, well, we are a bit criticized. You have overdone it. You have been too strong. Among friends we forgive, and we hope the friends will forgive us for what we have done, because the facts are speaking for themselves. And the facts speak for themselves by the miracles which happened in the land of miracles." Thus did Meridor with these and many other words give credit to God for the continued survival of the tiny nation of Israel.

PRIME MINISTER BEGIN

Begin recounted a history of Israel and the Jewish people's long struggles. He expressed hope that now a peace treaty could be signed with a new Lebanon. He added, "I can tell you something from my heart, thank God, we saved the Christians in Lebanon from the danger of physical destruction. Over 100,000 have been killed in the last seven years in Lebanon. Nobody wrote about this. The Christian population faced the danger of being completely annihilated. Now the Christians in Lebanon are safe. The PLO is defeated. We do not want one inch of Lebanese territory. We shall sign a peace treaty with Lebanon. Well, gentlemen, this is our hope, and on this happy note I would like to say, Shalom."

The following is an article in the *ON MAGAZINE*, 1982 Spring issue, on "A Date with Destiny—Menachem Begin":

The imminent demise of Menachem Begin seemed assured. In the winter of 1981, the Israeli Prime Minister's administration was under assault from every quarter. Inflation threatened the credibility of his economic program, diminishing his popularity among Israeli voters.

The Likud Coalition, which Begin had put together for the 1977 election, was fraying at the edges. Several of Begin's key people had left the government, protesting the foreign policy.

With the Likud bloc in disarray, the resurgent Labor Party, led by the confident Shimon Peres, felt assured of victory in the June election. The political prognosticators and the world press had already proclaimed Peres the newly-crowned prince of Israel. Both the United States and Egypt were delaying foreign policy initiatives until Peres assumed office.

However, the soothsayers of doom had given Begin his last rites far too early. The world press had failed to take several factors into account. They were unprepared for the spectacular economic initiatives of Begin's finance minister, Yoran Aridor, which took much of the impact of inflation away from the Israeli consumer. They were also unable to predict the sudden and violent turn of events in Lebanon which would showcase Begin's decisive leadership style. Most importantly, world opinion overlooked the character, personality and determination of Menachem Begin. When the smoke of the bitter 1981 campaign had cleared, the Likud Coalition of Menachem Begin had made a stunning comeback to squeak out a one-seat margin in the parliament. Once again Begin had kept his appointment with destiny.

Begin's conversation and thinking is dominated by his understanding of Israel's relationship to God. His entire life, he says, has been dedicated to the national salvation of Israel. In pursuit of this goal, he has gained an insight into suffering that few world leaders can claim to share. The holocaust he experienced as a youth in Poland during the Second World War burned in him the resolve that never again would the descendants of Abraham be subject to the fires of Buchenwald. Never again would the House of David face annihilation.

If there is a symbol of restoration for the people of Israel, and, in particular, Menachem Begin, it is Jerusalem, the "City of David." The psychological impact of the reunification during the 1967 Six Day War was so great that Israeli paratroopers broke down and wept when they approached the Wailing Wall. In the thinking of Begin, as well as the majority of the Jewish populace, Jerusalem is the ordained capital and has been since the time of David.

ISRAEL SHUNNED

Begin speaks about this divine right to the city in almost matter-of-fact terms, and sounds almost baffled when discussing the refusal of other nations to recognize Israel's claim to Jerusalem as its capital. "Every nation has its capital and all the other nations recognize that capital . . . the only one in the world which is not being recognized is Jerusalem," he states with a touch of bewilderment. He also

David Lewis with Prime Minister Begin, Jerusalem.

points out that in spite of a 1976 campaign resolution supporting Israel's claim to Jerusalem, the Carter Administration refused to transfer its Embassy to Jerusalem.

In 1947 the United Nations mandated there would be a state of Israel within certain boundaries. Ultimately, however, Begin is not concerned about UN mandates or world opinions. He claims his authority is from a higher source. Quoting his old rival, David Ben-Gurion, Begin said, "Some people say the mandate is our Bible; it is not so—the Bible is our mandate."

Besides Jerusalem, Begin feels Israel has a right to Judaea and Samaria (the "West Bank"), because of God's promise to Abraham in the book of Genesis. There can be no question, Begin contends, of preventing Israelis from settling on that land.

According to Begin, Israel's goal is to exercise its right to live in Judaea, Samaria and Gaza *together with its Arab inhabitants.* In "old" Israel (within the pre-1967 armistice lines) some 600,000 Arabs live today among some 3.5 million Jews. Begin states, "There should be no reason why 22,400 Jews should not reside among 700,000 Arabs in Judaea and Samaria."

Contrary to ABC's "20/20," Israeli officials claim there is no design to "drive the Palestinian Arabs off the land." "No Arabs have been deprived of their land or their livelihood," one high source says. The land on which Jewish towns and villages have been established is generally state land or ownerless tracts; invariably, moreover, it is uncultivated land.

Begin also balks at "20/20's" claim that "Arabs have worked this land for generations" and that the world is "witnessing the final phases of the liquidation of Palestine."

The UN partition of November 29, 1947, provided for the establishment of a "Palestinian" state. Although Israel accepted the partition, the Arabs rejected it and immediately went to war when Israel declared its independence. Jordan seized the "West Bank" and Egypt the Gaza Strip. Israel wonders why the world made no outcry for nineteen years that these areas should become an independent Palestinian state. Only since 1967 has this demand been heard.

A CONVERSATION WITH REAGAN

The Prime Minister related how he once inquired of Reagan, who was pressing him on the subject, what would happen to a governor in America who refused to allow a particular ethnic group to settle in a particular city. "Wouldn't that governor be accused of racism?" Begin asked. Following that same line of logic, Begin then asked, "How can I be expected to prevent my fellow citizens from settling in areas that are their birthright?" Begin insists that those settlements in no way infringe on the right of the indigenous Arabs currently living there, and that the Likud government is interested in protecting the rights of all its citizens.

A Palestinian state on the West Bank represents to Begin the greatest possible threat to Israel. Begin insists, "Such a Palestinian entity would be equivalent to a Soviet knife pointed right at the heart of both Israel and NATO." It seems absurd to Begin that western powers would claim to desire such a situation. He feels such a position is prompted by Saudi oil. Even so, understandably, Begin says, "The security of Israel is of far greater significance to me than is the plight of NATO."

EIGHT DEADLY MILES

If Israel returned to the pre-1967 borders, it would leave Israel with a stretch of land eight miles wide. This would allow Arab tanks to cut Israel in half. Begin imagines them saying, "Now we have 7,000 tanks. Soon we shall have 10,000, perhaps even 15,000 tanks. Then we shall attack and push them into the sea. Eight miles. *What is eight miles for a tank attack?*"

A tank attack is the greatest but not the only threat that Begin envisions from a Palestinian state. From the highlands of the West Bank, he says, *"It would be possible to hit every city in Israel with Russian-supplied rockets."* In addition, he is convinced that a Palestinian state would only serve to intensify terrorist activity. Begin's security forces broke up 142 PLO cells in 1980 which illustrates to him the necessity for maintaining military presence up to the Jordan River.

Nor is the Prime Minister persuaded by arguments that the creation of a Palestinian state would satisfy the legitimate aspirations of the Palestinian people, but remains convinced that the intent of establishing a separate state on the West Bank is to eventually push Israel into the sea.

The solution that Begin offers, and the one that he insists was agreed to at Camp David, is that of limited autonomy for the resident Palestinian population. Begin claims, "They will elect their own administrators but we have to reserve security." It is Begin's contention that Israeli sovereignty is best for all concerned; in particular, he insists that the West Bank natives receive more democratic treatment in the care of the Israeli government than was previously given by the Jordanian regime. Certain, Begin says, *"The Arabs receive better treatment from Israel than the Jews have been given at the hands of the Arabs in Arab countries."*

TWENTY-TWO VS. ONE

He views the Palestinian refugee problem as being created by the Arabs in order to "maintain a festering sore" to use against Israel. Furthermore, he does not see the problem in terms of Israeli and Palestinian, but rather, in terms of Jew and Arab. *The Arabs,* he maintains, *have twenty-two countries and the Jews only have one.* He implies that it is unfair for the Arabs to demand another country at the expense of Israeli territory. Begin willingly offers to provide assistance in working out a solution, but he insists the answer lies in resettlement within the sponsor countries and not in a mass remigration to Israel.

Begin maintains the hope for the future is tied to the belief that, ultimately, political events are Divinely ordered, and that the nation of Israel is central to God's plan. He is convinced that his nation's authority is derived from God. "The protection of my people rests not in the hands of American foreign policy but in Divine protection and in the tenacity of the citizens of Israel."

It is emblematic of powerful men that they are convinced that history will eventually vindicate them. However, few have as much faith in that vindication as Menachem Begin. His view of the universe is, in the final analysis, positive—remarkably so in light of his experience with the Holocaust. He remains convinced that, despite unending bloodshed and irreconcilable impasses, Truth will win out.

(1982) Briefing in Sidon with Major Saad Haddad (on right), Lewis (center), and Israeli officer (left).

Upon our return from Beirut, Isaac Rottenberg, Cal Thomas and I held a press conference attended by ABC-TV, United Press International, Kol Israel, and some reporters from various U.S. daily newspapers.

After this press conference, held in the Hilton Hotel of Jerusalem, Isaac and I were standing in the lobby of the Hilton. We spied a colleague, Jay Rawlings and greeted him. Jay began to tell us that while we were in the coastal area he was travelling for several days with a video camera team throughout all Lebanon, interviewing Palestinian people who live in the country. Here is part of the interview I then conducted with Jay. (Jay is the producer of the outstanding film *Apples of Gold*.)

LEWIS: "Did you talk to Palestinians as well as to the Lebanese people?"

RAWLINGS: "We talked to Palestinian people who had lived for 34 years in Lebanon. . . ."

LEWIS: "What is the attitude of the Palestinian people toward the PLO?"

RAWLINGS: "The Palestinians are tired of the fighting. They are tired of the problems they have been confronted with. They said to us personally that they only want to have freedom. They only want to live. They say that the PLO has fed them lies, and has given them false hope. No other human beings have had to suffer 34 years of being stateless people; people not able to travel; not given even second rate citizenship. They want to just live."

LEWIS: "You mention 'stateless people',—do they want a state?"

RAWLINGS: "The ones we talked to want to live in Lebanon where they have been living. Many of them have married Lebanese wives. Their children are Lebanese, as it were. They are not interested in carving up this country of Israel. They just want to live in peace and in harmony with their neighbors."

LEWIS: "You mean they want to be assimilated where they are?"

RAWLINGS: "Definitely."

LEWIS: "How did the Palestinians that you talked to view the Israeli entrance into Lebanon?"

RAWLINGS: "With great rejoicing, and great relief. We spoke to PLO captains, or *detainees* as they are called, men who were considered dangerous. They are being held in a camp in Southern Lebanon. We spoke to them and they said that they were sorry for what had happened. They were apologizing for the lies that they had been led to believe over the years. Now they are asking for forgiveness and the opportunity to live like normal human beings."

LEWIS: "Can you document what you are saying?"

RAWLINGS: "This has all been documented on video. It is presently being edited. I am getting all of this in Arabic translated to English. I will have this to give to the press, exactly their statements as they were given to me."

LEWIS: "The truth will be made available—if the world is ready to listen to the truth for a change."

RAWLINGS: "For a change."

Let us pray that men everywhere will open their minds and hearts to the truth—for a change.

13

CHRISTIAN LEADERSHIP CONFERENCE STATEMENT

Statement from visiting Christian delegation:

We have come to Israel and Lebanon as a group of Christians with membership in fifteen different denominations to listen and to look for ourselves. We have spoken with leaders in both countries, with people in the streets, as well as soldiers along the front lines. We have walked the streets of cities like Tyre and Sidon and have spoken with their residents.

After three days of extensive travel we have come to the conclusion that what we have seen and heard bears little resemblance to what we had been led to expect by some of the U.S. media. For instance, Tyre and Sidon are not destroyed cities, nor is Beirut. They are damaged cities, and this damage, caused mostly by the occupation and activities of the PLO represents a true tragedy in terms of human life, both Lebanese and Israeli. However, Tyre and Sidon are rapidly returning to normal; stores are doing a brisk business and most residents expressed to us their delight that the stranglehold of the PLO on their country has at last been broken.

Much of the destruction of Lebanon was caused by the PLO prior to the current Israeli operation. In Damor, for example, thousands of people were killed by the PLO and the city destroyed. We cannot help wondering why the world was silent while these atrocities were being committed. Criticism seems to be reserved for Israel alone.

While the basic intent of the Lebanese operation by Israel has been to secure the safe borders of Israel, a very significant side benefit has been the restoration of freedom to the Lebanese people. The nearly unanimous opinion of people we talked to at random on the street and in shops and stores was that the Lebanese are glad to be rid of the PLO and are grateful to Israel for breaking its grip on their country.

As we return to our 44 cities in 29 states, we intend to carry our support for Israel, reconfirmed by what we have seen and heard, and to communicate our observations to President Reagan, members of Congress, and to the media.

—National Christian Leadership Conference for Israel
Jerusalem, August 12, 1982

The statement was signed by the following members of the group:

Stuart Gaines, State Exec. Dir. MMOA, 1736 Merryvale Rd., Birmingham, AL 35216

Dr. Richard Vigneulle, Pastor & State Chairman, 2281 Old Tyler Rd., Birmingham, AL 35226

Rev. David Minor, Senior Pastor, 115 Beulah Drive, Longview, WA 98632

Rev. Robert J. Smith, Member Freeman Institute & Moral Majority Chairman Utah, Box 18596, Salt Lake City, UT 84118

Dr. Richard White, 9611 Seigen Lane, Baton Rouge, LA 70810

Mary A. Filben, 1537 Deerwood Drive E., Mobile, AL 36618

Paul J. Filben, Chairman Diocesar & International Affairs Commission, 1537 Deerwood Drive E., Mobile, AL 36618

Dr. Otto Reimherr, Prof. Emeritus, Susquehanna University, Selinsgrove, PA 17837

Bruce Peterson, P.O. Box 248, Schroon Lake, NY 12870

Rev. Robert L. Griese, 19 Fairlee Terrace, Waban, MA 02168

Rev. Dennis J. Brown, Pastor Yakima Bible Baptist Church, Dir. Moral Majority Washington, P.O. Box 167, Yakima, WA 98907

Dr. David A. Wood, Pastor Heritage Baptist Church, Chairman Moral Majority Michigan, P.O. Box 8214, Kentwood, MI 49508

Dr. R. Herbert Fitzpatrick, Pastor Baptist Church, Chairman Moral Majority Maryland, Upper Marlboro, MD 20772

Rev. Arthur S. Dones, Pastor St. Marks AME African Methodist Episcopal Church, 587 Springdale Avenue East, East Orange, NJ 07017

Rev. Robert P. Patterson, Baltimore, MD

Rev. Thomas P. Stewart, Buffalo, NY

Neil B. Blair, 3772 Little Rock Drive, Provo, UT 84057

Donnie Cantwell, Pastor Open Door Baptist Church, Chairman Moral Majority Virginia, 5327 Orcutt Lane, Richmond, VA

Jerry Prevo, Chairman Moral Majority Alaska, 6401 E. Northern Lights, Anchorage, AK 99504

Dr. Jack Wyrtzen, President, Word of Life Bible Institute, Schroon Lake, NY 12870

Dr. Richard C. Lux, Assoc. Prof. Scripture & Adv. Com. Catholic Jewish Relations NCCB, Sacred Heart School of Theology, 3264 N. Summit, Milwaukee, WI 53211

Dr. Paul G. Cunningham, Senior Pastor College Church of the Nazarene, 2020 E. Sheridan, Olathe, KS 66062

Clayton B. Simmons, Vice Chairman Moral Majority North Carolina, 3216 Stoneyford Court, Raleigh, NC 27603

William T. Monroe, Pastor Florence Baptist Temple, Chairman Moral Majority South Carolina, 2308 S. Irby Street, Florence, SC 29501

Lamarr Mooneyham, Chairman Moral Majority North Carolina, 4024 Pope Road, Durham, NC 27707

Roy McLaughlin, Pastor First Baptist Church, Chairman Moral Majority Arkansas, Route 2, Box 23, Vilonia, AR 72173

C. D. Walker, Director of Missions, Baptist Missionary Associate of Texas, Box 4146, Dallas, TX 75208

Isaac Rottenberg, Executive Director NCLCI, 134 E. 39th Street, New York, NY 10016

Herbert M. Freedholm, President, Ministerium, Bethesta Covenant Church, 118 Washington St., Rockford, IL 61108

Marvin Eiklor, President Shalom Fellowship, Box 582, Keene, NH 03431

Marvin R. Wilson, Professor of Biblical Studies, Gordon College, Wenham, MA 01984

Robert R. Kyte, Pastor United Church of Christ, Lenox, MA 01240

C. Philip Hinerman, Pastor Park Avenue United Methodist Church, 3400 Park Avenue, Minneapolis, MN 554071

John D. Morgan, Pastor Sagement Baptist Church, 11323 Hughes Road, Houston, TX 77089

Tom Trammel, Pastor Deer Park Baptist Church, 3225 Plateau Pl., Cincinnati, OH 45241

Wayne Cress, Chairman Moral Majority Ohio, 2956 Cleveland Avenue, Columbus, OH 43224

Billy Joe Daughterty, Pastor Victory Christian Centre, 4400 S. Sheridan, Tulsa, OK 74129

James R. Lyons, The Ecumenical Institute for Jewish-Christian Studies, 26275 Northwestern Highway, Southfield, MI 48076

Donald J. Wold, Institute for Jewish Christian Relations, 1318½ Havenhurst Drive, Suite 15, Los Angeles, CA 90046

H. W. Barnett, Pastor Victorin Tabernacle, 1500 Central Avenue, Kansas City, KS 66102

Tommy Barnett, Pastor First Assembly of God, 2025 North 3rd Street, Phoenix, AZ 85004

Dr. Greg Dixon, Pastor, Indianapolis Baptist Temple, Moral Majority National Secretary, 2635 S.E. St., Indianapolis, Ind. 46241

J. I. Morriss, Rocky Mountain Fellowship, P.O. Box 302, Littleton, CO 80123

Clarence H. Wagner, Jr., President, Executive Director Bridges for Peace, P.O. Box 33145, Tulsa, OK 74135 USA, or P.O. Box 7304, Jerusalem, Israel

David A. Lewis, President, National Christian Leadership Conference for Israel, 304 E. Manchester, Springfield, MO 65807

14

BACK HOME TO THE USA

We arrived in New York on August 12. Rottenberg, Rev. Arthur Jones (Methodist pastor) and I were met by a TV crew from WOR Channel 9. This was a very good news conference. As I watched it on the Noon Report in New York I was satisfied that they had selected the best parts of the lengthy interview, giving us quite a bit of time, and presenting a fair case for what we had to say. The report from WOR-TV 9 told me that they are also the Independent News Network and go out by cable to 40 states.

On August 14 I gave a 45-minute interview, live, via phone for a radio station in Carlinville, Illinois, Station WIBI. I was interviewed by Bill Snyder. Later the same day I was interviewed by our local TV stations Channels 3 and 27 (both in Springfield, Missouri). Both used segments of the interview in the news. Also interviewed by the Springfield **LEADER PRESS** (daily newspaper) we got front page (top of the page) coverage, and a good article in the Sunday paper. That evening I was interviewed by TV Channel 10, and also got good coverage there on local news.

It was my privilege to speak for Pastor Albert Calloway at Park Crest Assembly of God on the 15th of August, where we distributed many copies of the **JERUSALEM COURIER** that we publish. On August 21, I spoke to the Full Gospel Business Men's monthly dinner meeting. The place was packed out with many people standing.

We review this merely to show you that it is possible to get the truth out to the public. We have gotten some hate mail, even some death threats, but the majority of response has been positive. We are beginning to get reports from the NCLCI New York Office (Rottenberg, our Executive Director) and directly from some of the participants in the trip to Lebanon. It seems that many of the men are having good success. Tommy Barnett did a two-hour interview when he got home to Phoenix. Richard Lux had a very good interview in the **MILWAUKEE SENTINAL**, a copy of which I just received.

PRESS COMES TO ITS SENSES

As more and more of us come back with a true report, an eyewitness report, more and more reporters are beginning to realize that if they ever want any credibility they had better start looking at things more objectively. We wrote in a previous chapter of Chancellor's change.

Many others, such as Jack Anderson, surprised us with some very fair and objective articles. Anderson never been perceived as being a particular friend of Israel, nevertheless wrote an editorial, "Palestinian Guerrillas are Miscast as Heroes of Beirut." In this article he wrote:

Columnist James J. Kilpatrick wrote an editorial, "Blood On the Hands of Yashir Arafat." He said,

For the past two months, night after night on the evening TV news, all of us have gazed in dismay upon the suffering in Lebanon—the dead, the wounded, the homeless—and night after night the same implicit message has flashed subliminally across the screen: **THE ISRAELIS ARE RESPONSIBLE FOR THIS**.

It is high time, it seems to me, to put the lie to this insidious nonsense. Let us place the blame for the destruction and bloodshed squarely where it belongs, upon the shoulders of that smirking monster with the manic grin on his face, Yashir Arafat, leader of the Palestine Liberation Organization.

Israel has no quarrel with the Palestinian Arabs as a people. Israel's rage is directed at that formless, shapeless nonentity of an entity, the Palestine Liberation Organization. The PLO has none of the trappings of sovereignty or statehood, but it is treated as a sovereign state. The PLO's chieftain swaggers to the United Nations to address the nations of the world; the PLO maintains an army supplied and equipped by the Soviet Union; here in the United States we talk constantly of "recognizing" the PLO.

WHO IS TO BLAME for the suffering in Beirut? Who prolongs the agony? The PLO moved into this beautiful and inoffensive city like a gangster mob, terrorizing the inhabitants. Aided and abetted by the Soviet Union, the PLO made Beirut a headquarters for international terrorism. With its stunning defeat at the hands of Israeli troops, the PLO reacted in the most cowardly and contemptible fashion: The PLO took the civilians of Lebanon as hostages, and hid behind them while it stalled for time.

It is objected that Israel had promised to use its U.S. arms for defensive purposes only. One response is that, given the relentless nature of the PLO's threat, the best defense is a good offense. In these past eight weeks, the Israelis have done us a tremendous favor: they have demonstrated in ways that war "games" could never demonstrate, the superiority of American planes, tanks and other weapons. It is not only the PLO that has been humiliated; it is the Soviet Union also.

After a scathing denunciation of John Chancellor's earlier position R. Emmet Tyrrell Jr. writes in the **NEW YORK POST**:

The PLO is a criminal organization. In 1972 its henchmen invaded Munich's Olympic village and slaughtered 11 unarmed Israeli athletes.

In 1974 the PLO seized a schoolhouse in Maalot, Israel, held over 100 captive and murdered 20.

In 1978 it waylaid a Tel Aviv bus and massacred 33 civilians.

It has done much more. It has fired SAM missiles at commercial aircraft.

It has hijacked the planes of at least eight world airlines.

The civil war it precipitated to gain control of Lebanon left over 100,000 dead.

So far as I know, the PLO is the only political organization on earth that as a matter of policy eschews battle with its enemies' soldiers for attacking its enemies' civilians. Now Israel has cornered these dreadful killers, and is being diabolized.

The PLO has taken refuge in a neutral city, and has used civilians as shields. Faced with defeat it utters blood-curdling oaths. Nonetheless, influential Americans even in the Reagan Administration urge negotiations.

Such Americans live in blissful isolation. Cushioned by vast oceans and by friendly nations north and south, insolated by American affluence, they do not appreciate the depth of the enmities that exist in this world.

Yet the enemies of Western democracy are today more violent, blatant and ubiquitous than were the prewar Fascists and Nazis. Moreover, Americans can now see some of their enemies' most wicked deeds on television as they take place.

We are up against an isolationism more profound than that of the 1930's . . . and less excusable.

Rottenberg writes to the NEW YORK TIMES: MIDDLE EAST: THE WORLD'S BELATED OUTRAGE

To the Editor:

In his July 24 Op-Ed article, "Beirut's Smell of Death," Kevin M. Cahill vividly describes the horrors of war and wonders about the harvest of hatred. As a Christian supporter of Israel, I share his horror at the sight of maimed bodies and uprooted lives. But I also detect a good deal of hypocrisy in much of the weeping and wailing that is going on right now.

Many of us have warned for years that the winds were being sown and that the whirlwinds would eventually have to be reaped. Some of the people who now scream the loudest were silent then.

For decades, Israeli peace overtures were met with an Arab trinity of negatives: no recognition, no negotiation, no reconcilliation. Some of the most ominous threats against the Jewish state were brushed aside by many people, including associates of mine in the Christian bureaucracy, as "mere rhetoric," and Jewish concerns were attributed to an understandable but exaggerated "Holocaust complex."

The coldblooded murders of civilians, athletes and air travelers by terrorists in order to "call attention to the plight of the Palestinian people" were described as acts that should not be condoned but that were understandable in light of Arab frustrations. Rarely were we treated to the detailed descriptions of torn limbs and shattered bodies in the accounts of those atrocities.

The Arab states, despite their immense wealth, have let Palestinians rot away in camps precisely because those camps served as schools of hatred where children

Isaac Rottenberg, Executive Director, NCLCI

were indoctrinated in the tenets of the PLO covenant. The world stood by and preferred not to think to much about the whirlwinds of misery that all this hatred would eventually produce, not least for those who were trained to be haters.

I very much want to believe that the unholy trinity of negatives will be replaced by a policy of recognition, negotiations and reconciliation. But I don't blame the Israelis if they want to see much clearer evidence of a real change of heart before they risk their very survival. It seems to me that the Palestinian problem, including the problem of resolving it, must be seen in the wider context of the inability of most of the Arab world to reconcile itself to any Israeli presence in the Middle East.

Millions of Christians will continue to support Israel, not because they are insensitive to suffering or wish to glorify Israeli military exploits, but because they honestly believe that the harvest of hatred could one day again mean a threat to the survival of the Jewish people. They may have their disagreements with Prime Minister Begin, but they identify with him when he says, "Never again."

—Isaac C. Rottenberg
Executive Director, National Christian
Leadership Conference for Israel
New York, July 26, 1982

LEWIS INTERVIEWED BY LEADER PRESS

Israelis seen as "Liberators"

The Israelis are more eager to leave Lebanon than the Lebanese people are to see them leave, says the Rev. David Lewis, who headed a delegation of Christians to Lebanon and Israel last week.

While the basic intent of the Israeli invasion of Lebanon has been to secure Israel's borders, an added benefit of the military action has been the liberation of the Lebanese people from the PLO, said Rev. Lewis, president of the National Christian Leadership Conference for Israel.

Lewis, an ordained Assemblies of God minister who lives in Springfield, said he organized the fact-finding mission because he and other Christians thought the U.S. media was not giving a fair shake to the Israeli position.

The group of 56 Christian leaders representing 15 denominations visited Israel and Lebanon, including the besieged capitol city of Beirut, and attended a meeting of Israel's parliament during their trip last week. Lewis said he met privately with Israeli Prime Minister Menachem Begin before the prime minister briefed the entire delegation.

"The Israelis are going through an agonizing time in the moral assessment of what they're doing," he said of his impressions after meeting with Begin.

"It is a source of agony for Begin that the problem of the Palestinians exists," he said. "But the covenant of the PLO calls for the destruction of the Jewish state and Israel cannot negotiate with terrorists who swear to its destruction."

Contrary to the impressions that the news media has created, he said, the majority of Lebanese and Palestinian people with whom the members of the fact-finding mission talked said they were grateful to Israel for breaking the PLO's grip on their country.

"Almost universally, we didn't hear any one of the people we stopped say anything other than that," Lewis said. "They said, 'We welcome the Israelis as liberators.' "

When they asked the people if they would like all foreign forces to leave, Lewis said, they replied that they wished the Syrians and PLO would get out immediately but that they needed the Israelis to help them restructure their government.

The delegation is not convinced that the PLO is the desired representative of the Palestinian people. "If given the opportunity, they would choose someone else to represent," Lewis said, mentioning the mayors of several Lebanese cities as possible leaders.

Almost 60 percent of the South Lebanon Christian enclave, a protective militia against the PLO, are Moslem, he said.

Lewis believes peace is possible but only if all the parties involved "recognize that Israel is going to exist and that the Palestinians are among the most mistreated people in history."

In his three-step peace plan, Lewis said, the Arab nations must first recognize Israel's right to exist, then work out a peace treaty and finally negotiate a solution to the plight of the Palestinian refugees.

"If I wasn't an idealist, I'd say it's hopeless," Lewis said. "I'm pro-Israel, but I'm not anti-anyone. I believe God desires that peace should exist."

Israel can act as a catalyst for peace by bringing everyone to the table, he said. The solution can be arranged with a new Lebanese government—not by returning the Palestinians to their homeland, but by assimilation throughout other Arab countries.

Why can't the Palestinians be allowed to return to the homes they were forced from when Israel became a state? Lewis paused as he considers that question. "There is no fairness in the world," he replied.

Among other conclusions the group made after three days of travel in the Lebanon was that the media has exaggerated the extent of damage inflicted by the Israelis.

With the exception of heavy damage in West Beirut, most of the destruction in other Lebanese cities like Tyre and Sidon was caused by the PLO before the Israeli offensive, he said. Only the city of Damor is destroyed.

"The Lebanese people are very aggressive and very industrious," he said. "They are already rebuilding. Everywhere you go you see building cranes and workers clearing away rubble."

The group learned that Israel uncovered massive underground bunkers of armaments—"enough to supply a massive modern army of hundreds of thousands of men," Lewis said.

"We had tentative reports of this and got confirmation Israel feels that, very possibly, the PLO was planning an invasion of Israel by bringing in Angolans and Cubans. Already a significant percentage of the PLO are not Arabs. Many are east Europeans and the whole thing is being orchestrated from Moscow."

By Julie Westermann
The News-Leader

A correction must be made relating to the Springfield **LEADER PRESS** article. I was not the organizer of the trip to Lebanon. The work was done by our executive secretary and by Cal Thomas who works for Jerry Falwell. The reporter assumed that I was the organizer of the trip because of my name being listed in the **NEW YORK TIMES** advertisement (which I gave to her) as the President of NCLCI. Since NCLCI sponsored the trip she assumed that I was the one who put it together. I do not want to detract from the fine work done by Cal and Isaac, each of whom enlisted 28 of the participants on the Lebanon trip, of which I was privileged to be a part.

15

WHAT WE WANT IN LEBANON

An Israeli Speaks

By Moshe Arens, Israel's Ambassador to the United States

Israel is interested in and prepared for the cessation of all hostilities in Lebanon as soon as possible. In fact, were it not for the intervention of the Syrians in the past 48 hours, our drive against the terrorists would have been completed upon attaining our stated objective: "to place all the civilian population of the Galilee beyond the range of terrorist fire."

It has surely not gone unnoticed that while various nations have suffered what President Reagan has himself called "the scourge of terrorism" and others have recognized its evil face, only Israel has been ready to take up the challenge and actually confront the danger and endeavor to erase it at the cost of valuable young lives.

In doing so, we have exercised our legitimate right of self-defense under Article 51 of the United Nations Charter.

The population in the north of our country was subject to bombardment from terrorist emplacements within neighboring Lebanon, whose government lost control of the situation more than seven years ago. They deliberately placed their guns in centers of the Lebanese civilian population, expecting them to derive immunity and to perpetrate their constant aggression with impunity. It is our concerned belief that no nation, forced to live under the circumstances of our northern population, would act differently.

For as long as it was possible, we willingly cooperated with the political efforts of Ambassador Philip Habib. But even his consummate diplomatic skill was unable to restrain the PLO terrorists for long. Since July 1981, when he achieved the cessation of hostilities, the terrorists had violated their commitment nearly 150 times in a chain of events that culminated in the attempted assassination of our ambassador to London, Shlomo Argov.

Following upon this record of barbarism, our defense forces were ordered to sweep the PLO terrorists out of southern Lebanon, to destroy their guns and put them beyond the reach of our population. This meant creating a PLO-free zone approximately 40 kilometers deep. Obviously, to attain that and for tactical and topographical reasons, our forces were obliged to move temporarily further north in some parts of the terrain.

The presence of a large Syrian force in unhappy Lebanon is a complicating factor. At the start of our action, we declared that we would not attack the Syrians unless forced to do so in self-defense. Prime Minister Begin urged the Syrian leaders to stay out of our conflict with the PLO. They are, after all, not there as the PLO's guardians.

To our regret, the Syrians did not heed our request, nor our warnings but became actively engaged in ground and air combat with our forces. As a result, the fighting has spread, and the operation, which we wanted to limit in time and in scope, has been extended.

We have not abandoned hope that wiser counsel will prevail in Damascus and that the Assad government will order its troops to disengage and, better still, to leave Lebanon.

It is my earnest desire to emphasize that we are not at war with the people of Lebanon, who are the unfortunate victims of unnecessary, unjustified and prolonged occupation by numerous foreign military elements, principally the PLO and the Syrians.

We do not covet a square inch of Lebanese soil and have no intention of remaining there a minute longer than necessary. We are anxious to see the emergence of a free, secure Lebanon whose territorial integrity we would respect and with whom we would gladly conclude a peace treaty.

Since the commencement of our struggle against the PLO, we have received innumerable messages of good will and expressions of support from Americans in all parts of this great country. None has moved me more than one from a Lebanese who states that "having been obliged to leave my country because of the Syrian/Palestinian occupation and the destruction of my country, I would like to express my gratitude to the Israeli people and army for their intervention in Lebanon and the help they are giving us for the restoration of our pride and independence."

Israeli Ambassador Moshe Arens receives a copy of "ON Magazine" from David Lewis. The cover article about Prime Minister Begin was written by David Lewis.

"I think that only a people who suffered understands the suffering the Lebanese people went through these seven years of tyranny. I only hope that this war will end as soon as possible in order to avoid more death and destruction. Thank you again, and God bless your people and each one of your soldiers."

A dramatic change in the fortunes of Lebanon will only be possible when the PLO ceases to be a factor in that country, as it is not a factor in any other independent Arab state.

Therefore, it is in the mutual interest of Israel and Lebanon for our present operation to go its normal course to a successful conclusion, which means that the terrorists will not be permitted to threaten both our peoples from that territory.

A revived, independent Lebanon, at peace with neighboring Israel, free of the PLO terrorists and the Syrian-Soviet surrogates, would be a boon to all the free world. This historic opportunity for positive change should be grasped by the United States.

16

THE REAGAN RESPONSE

Wednesday, September 1, 1982, was a night of shocking revelation for those of us who love and support Israel. The President made a speech that was immediately perceived by the Israeli's to be hostile. Many of us wondered at President Reagan's new direction. As he condemned Israel's settlements on the West Bank we remembered that he had previously said, while Jimmy Carter was president, "The present administration in Washington is dead wrong when it says Israel's West Bank settlements are illegal." Later he said, "Jewish and Arab Palestinians have a right to settle there until Jordan and Israel between them decide on secure and recognized borders."

Why had he so radically changed his mind? Was his anger toward Prime Minister Menechem Begin so strong as to promote this reaction? Was he punishing Israel?

Here is the entire text of Ronald Reagan's speech:

Burbank, Calif., Sept. 1 (AP)—following is the prepared text of President Reagan's speech tonight on the Middle East, as issued here by the White House:

Today has been a day that should make all of us proud. It marked the end of the successful evacuation of the PLO from Beirut, Lebanon. This peaceful step could never have been taken without the good offices of the United States and, especially, the truly heroic work of a great American diplomat, Ambassador Philip Habib. Thanks to his efforts, I am happy to announce that the U.S. Marine contingent helping to supervise the evacuation has accomplished its mission. Our young men should be out of Lebanon within two weeks. They, too, have served the cause of peace with distinction and we can all be very proud of them.

But the situation in Lebanon is only part of the overall problem of conflict in the Middle East. So, over the past two weeks, while events in Beirut dominated the front page, America was engaged in a quiet, behind-the-scenes effort to lay the groundwork for a broader peace in the region. For once, there were no premature leaks as U.S. diplomatic missions traveled to Mideast capitals and I met here at home with a wide range of experts to map out an American peace initiative for the long-suffering peoples of the Middle East, Arab and Israeli alike.

It seemed to me that, with the agreement in Lebanon, we had an opportunity for a more far-reaching peace effort in the region and I was determined to seize that moment. In the words of the Scripture, the time had come to "follow after the things which make for peace."

Tonight, I want to report to you on the steps we have taken, and the prospects they can open up for a just and lasting peace in the Middle East.

America has long been committed to bring peace to this troubled region. For more than a generation, successive U.S. administrations have endeavored to develop a fair and workable process that could lead to a true and lasting Arab-Israeli peace. Our involvement in the search for Mideast peace is not a matter of preference, it is a moral imperative. The strategic importance of the region to the U.S. is well known.

But our policy is motivated by more than strategic interests. We also have an irreversible commitment to the survival and territorial integrity of friendly states. Nor can we ignore the fact that the well-being of much of the world's economy is tied to stability in the strife-torn Middle East. Finally, our traditional humanitarian concerns dictate a continuing effort to peacefully resolve conflicts.

Following Predecessors' Lead

When our Administration assumed office in January 1981, I decided that the general framework for our Middle East policy should follow the broad guidelines laid down by our predecessors.

There were two basic issues we had to address. First, there was the strategic threat to the region posed by the Soviet Union and its surrogates, best demonstrated by the brutal war in Afghanistan; and, second, the peace process between Israel and its Arab neighbors. With regard to the Soviet threat, we have strengthened our efforts to develop with our friends and allies a joint policy to deter the Soviets and their surrogates from further expansion in the region, and, if necessary, to defend against it. With respect to the Arab-Israeli conflict, we have embraced the Camp David framework as the only way to proceed. We have also recognized, however, that solving the Arab-Israeli conflict, in and of itself, cannot assure peace throughout a region as vast and troubled as the Middle East.

Our first objective under the Camp David process was to insure the successful fulfillment of the Egyptian-Israeli peace treaty. This was achieved with the peaceful return to the Sinai to Egypt in April 1982. To accomplish this, we worked hard with our Egyptian and Israeli friends, and eventually with other friendly countries, to create the multinational force which now operates in the Sinai.

Throughout this period of difficult and time-consuming negotiations, we never lost sight of the next step of Camp David, autonomy talks to pave the way for permitting the Palestinian people to exercise their legitimate rights. However, owing to the tragic assassination of President Sadat and other crises in the area, it was not until January 1982 that we were able to make a major effort to renew these talks. Secretary of State Haig and Ambassador Fairbanks made three visits to Israel and Egypt this year to pursue the autonomy talks. Considerable progress was made in developing the basic outline of an American approach which was to be presented to Egypt and Israel after April.

The successful completion of Israel's withdrawal from Sinai and the courage shown on this occasion by Prime Minister Begin and President Mubarak in living up to their agreements convinced me the time had come for a new American policy to try to bridge the remaining differences between Egypt and Israel in the autonomy process. So, in May, I called for specific measures and a timetable for consultations with the Governments of Egypt and Israel on the next steps in the peace process. However, before this effort could be launched, the conflict in Lebanon pre-empted our efforts. The autonomy talks were basically put on hold while we sought to untangle the parties in Lebanon and still the guns of war.

New Opportunity for Peace

The Lebanon war, tragic as it was, has left us with a new opportunity for Middle East peace. We must seize it now and bring peace to this troubled area so vital to world stability while there is still time. It was with this strong conviction that over a month ago, before the present negotiations in Beirut had been completed, I directed Secretary of State Shultz to again review our policy and to consult a wide range of outstanding Americans on the best ways to strengthen chances for peace in the Middle East.

We have consulted with many of the officials who were historically involved in the process, with members of the congress, and with individuals from the private sector, and I have held extensive consultations with my own advisers on the principles I will outline to you tonight.

The evacuation of the PLO from Beirut is now complete. And we can now help the Lebanese to rebuild their war-torn country. We owe it to ourselves, and to posterity, to move quickly to build up this achievement. A stable and revived Lebanon is essential to all our hopes for peace in the region. The people of Lebanon deserve the best efforts of the international community to turn the nightmares of the past several years into a new dawn of hope.

But the opportunities for peace in the Middle East do not begin and end in Lebanon. As we help Lebanon rebuild, we must also move to resolve the root causes of conflict between Arabs and Israelis.

The war in Lebanon has demonstrated many things, but two consequences are key to the peace process:

First, the military losses of the PLO have not diminished the yearning of the Palestinian people for a just solution of their claims; and second, while Israel's military successes in Lebanon have demonstrated that its armed forces are second to none in the region, they alone cannot bring just and lasting peace to Israel and her neighbors.

The question now is how to reconcile Israel's legitimate security concerns with the legitimate rights of the Palestinians. And that answer can only come at the negotiating table. Each party must recognize that the outcome must be acceptable to all and that true peace will require compromises by all.

Fresh Start Needed in Region

So, tonight I am calling for a fresh start. This is the moment for all those directly concerned to get involved—to lend their support—to a workable basis for peace. The Camp David agreement remains the foundation of our policy. Its language provides all parties with the leeway they need for successful negotiations.

I call on Israel to make clear that the security for which she yearns can only be achieved through genuine peace, a peace requiring magnanimity, vision and courage.

I call on the Palestinian people to recognize that their own political aspirations are inextricably bound to recognition of Israel's right to a secure future.

And I call on the Arab states to accept the reality of Israel, and the reality that peace and justice are to be gained only through hard, fair, direct negotiation.

In making these calls upon others, I recognize that the United States has a special responsibility. No other nation is in a position to deal with the key parties to the conflict on the basis of trust and reliability.

The time has come for a new realism on the part of all the peoples of the Middle East. The State of Israel is an accomplished fact; it deserves unchallenged legitimacy within the community of nations. But Israel's legitimacy has thus far been recognized by too few countries, and has been denied by every Arab state except Egypt. Israel exists; it has a right to demand of its neighbors that they recognize those facts.

The war in Lebanon has demonstrated another reality in the region. The departure of the Palestinians from Beirut dramatizes more than ever the homelessness of the Palestinian people. Palestinians feel strongly that their cause is more than a question of refugees. I agree. The Camp David agreement recognized that fact when it spoke of the legitimate rights of the Palestinian people and their just requirements. For peace to endure, it must involve all those who have been most deeply affected by the conflict. Only through broader participation in the peace process, most immediately by Jordan and by the Palestinians, will Israel be able to rest confident in the knowledge that its security and integrity will be respected by its neighbors. Only through the process of negotiation can all the nations of the Middle East achieve a secure peace.

These then are our general goals. What are the specific new American positions, and why are we taking them?

In the Camp David talks thus far, both Israel and Egypt have felt free to express openly their views as to what the outcome should be. Understandably, their views have differed on many points.

U.S. Role as Mediator

The United States has thus far sought to play the role of mediator. We have avoided public comment on the key issues. We have always recognized, and continue to recognize, that only the voluntary agreement of those parties most directly involved in the conflict can provide an enduring solution. But it has become evident to me that some clearer sense of America's position on the key issues is necessary to encourage wider support for the peace process.

First, as outlined in the Camp David accords, there must be a period of time during which the Palestinian inhabitants of the West Bank and Gaza will have full autonomy over their own affairs. Due consideration must be given to the principles of self-government by the inhabitants of the territories and to the legitimate security concerns of the parties involved.

The purpose of the five-year period of transition which would begin after free elections for a self-governing Palestinian authority is to prove to the Palestinians that they can run their own affairs, and that such Palestinian automony poses no threat to Israel's security.

The United States will not support the use of any additional land for the purpose of settlements during the transition period. Indeed, the immediate adoption of a settlement freeze by Israel, more than any other action, could create the confidence needed for wider participation in these talks. Further settlement activity is in no way necessary for the security of Israel and only diminishes the confidence of the Arabs that a final outcome can be freely and fairly negotiated.

I want to make the American position clearly understood: The purpose of this transition period is the peaceful and orderly transfer of domestic authority from Israel to the Palestinian inhabitants of the West Bank and Gaza. At the same time, such a transfer must not interfere with Israel's security requirements.

Beyond the transition period, as we look to the future of the West Bank and Gaza, it is clear to me that peace cannot be achieved by the formation of an independent Palestinian state in those territories. Nor is it achievable on the basis of Israeli sovereignty or permanent control over the West Bank and Gaza.

So the United States will not support the establishment of an independent Palestinian state in the West Bank and Gaza, and we will not support annexation or permanent control by Israel.

Jordan Role in West Bank

There is, however, another way to peace. The final status of these lands must, of course, be reached through the give-and-take of negotiations. But it is the firm view of the United States that self-government by the Palestinians of the West Bank and Gaza in association with Jordan offers the best chance for a durable, just and lasting peace.

We base our approach squarely on the principle that the Arab-Israeli conflict should be resolved through negotiations involving an exchange of territory for peace. This exchange is enshrined in United Nations Security Council Resolution 242, which is, in turn, incorporated in all its parts in the Camp David agreements. U.N. Resolution 242 remains wholly valid as the foundation stone of America's Middle East peace effort.

It is the United States' position that—in return for peace—the withdrawal provision of Resolution 242 applies to all fronts, including the West Bank and Gaza.

When the border is negotiated between Jordan and Israel, our view on the extent to which Israel should be asked to give up territory will be heavily affected by the extent of true peace and normalization and the security arrangements offered in return.

Finally, we remain convinced that Jerusalem must remain undivided, but its final status should be decided through negotiations.

In the course of the negotiations to come, the United States will support positions that seem to us fair and reasonable compromises, and likely to promote a sound agreement. We will also put forward our own detailed proposals when we believe they can be helpful. And, make no mistake, the United States will oppose any proposal—from any party and at any point in the negotiating process—that threatens the security of Israel. America's commitment to the security of Israel is ironclad.

During the past few days, our Ambassadors in Israel, Egypt, Jordan, and Saudi Arabia have presented to their host governments the proposals in full detail that I have outlined here tonight.

I am convinced that these proposals can bring justice, bring security and bring durability to an Arab-Israeli peace.

The United States will stand by these principles with total dedication. They are fully consistent with Israel's security requirements and the aspirations of the Palestinians. We will work hard to broaden participation at the peace table as envisaged by the Camp David accords. And I fervently hope that the Palestinians and Jordan, with the support of their Arab colleagues, will accept this opportunity.

Conflict a Threat to World

Tragic turmoil in the Middle East runs back to the dawn of history. In our modern day, conflict after conflict has taken its brutal toll there. In an age of nuclear challenge and economic interdependence, such conflicts are a threat to all the people of the world, not just the Middle East itself. It is time for us all, in the Middle East and around the world, to call a halt to conflict, hatred and prejudice; it is time for us all to launch a common effort for reconstruction, peace and progress.

It has often been said—and regretably too often been true—that the story of the search for peace and justice in the Middle East is a tragedy of opportunities missed.

In the aftermath of the settlement in Lebanon we now face an opportunity for a broader peace. This time we must not let it slip from our grasp. We must look beyond the difficulties and obstacles of the present and move with fairness and resolve toward a brighter future. We owe it to ourselves, and to posterity, to do no less. For if we miss this chance to make a fresh start, we may look back on this moment from some later vantage point and realize how much that failure cost us all.

These, then, are the principles upon which American policy towards the Arab-Israeli conflict will be based. I have made a personal commitment to see that they endure and, God willing, that they will come to be seen by all reasonable, compassionate people as fair, achievable, and in the interests of all who wish to see peace in the Middle East.

Tonight, on the eve of what can be a dawning of new hope for the people of the troubled Middle East—and for all the world's people who dream of a just and peaceful future—I ask you, my fellow Americans, for your support and your prayers in this great undertaking.

What wonder filled our minds as we listened. We trembled, for the Word of God promises to bless those who bless the seed of Jacob (Israel) and CURSE THOSE WHO CURSE ISRAEL. What will happen to our beloved nation if we abandon Israel?

On the next day after the speech I called Isaac Rottenberg and Rev. William Harter (Secretary-Treasurer of NCLCI). We conferred with other executive members and jointly produced the following statement for the press:

Christian Leaders Respond to President Reagan's Middle East Approach

We commend President Reagan for his sincere desire to bring peace to the troubled Middle East. Furthermore, we appreciate the President's expression of his personal commitment to the security of Israel.

However, we are deeply troubled both by the policies President Reagan now seems to be enunciating and the process that is being followed in dealing with extremely sensitive Middle East issues. The dramatic gesture in which the President of the United States predetermines what the outcome of negotiations ought to be, can only lead to tension with our ally Israel on the one hand and false expectations about U.S. guaranteed quick solutions on the other hand. The end result will be that once again a military victory by Israel against its enemies is being turned into a diplomatic disadvantage, designed to portray Israel as the major obstacle to peace in the region. We believe that this approach is both unfair and counterproductive.

Jordan, whose illegal annexation of the West Bank after the 1948 war was recognized only by Great Britain and Pakistan, should not now be rewarded by the United

States with territory to which it has no historic rights. On the other hand, we express the profound hope that Jordan will soon join the negotiations for a just settlement of the Palestinian problem. The opportunities for a peace agreement between Israel and Jordan which will benefit both nations as well as the Palestinian Arabs are now greater than ever.

—The Executive Committee
NCLCI

While a candidate for the presidency Mr. Reagan had spoken out clearly as a friend of Israel. He said, "Israel has the democratic will, the national cohesiveness and stability, the technological capacity and military fiber to stand forth as a trusted and MUCH NEEDED ALLY." He often repeated that message.

The President also rejected any heavy-handed pressure on Israel in negotiating a peace for the region. He stated, "We will not impose a settlement on either Israel or the Arab states. A Reagan Administration will not force the hand of either Israel or Egypt at the negotiating table."

Candidate Reagan wrote a column in which he said, "Specific Arab states such as Egypt, friendly to us at a particular moment, may well be able and prepared to take a front-line position in defense of Western interest. To the extent that one or more can participate, so much the better. But such secondary links cannot substitute for a strong Israel." He promised that this administration "would not continue to ship massive quantities of sophisticated armaments to so-called 'moderate' Arab states who, in fact, might directly threaten Israel's existence." But then came the AWACS, and now this. We can only wonder WHAT NEXT?

On the subject of Jerusalem, Mr. Reagan declared, "I believe that we could, recognizing the rights of people to go to their holy places of other religions there, have the sovereignty of an undivided Jerusalem *be that of Israel.*"

Concerning the Palestinian dilemma, Mr. Reagan said

that the blame should not be placed on Israel but on the Arab nations that refused a solution and resettlement of the Palestinians. He repeatedly branded the PLO as a terrorist organization that had one purpose and that was the destruction of Israel. Mr. Reagan said, "There never was a Palestinian nation. There was a Palestine area and it was a mandate under the British and when the British set out to make a nation, the British created Jordan with 80% of what land had been called Palestine." Concerning the Refugee problem he stated, "One solution to this refugee problem could be assimilation in Jordan. DESIGNATED BY THE U.N. AS THE ARAB PALESTINIAN STATE."

Here is the text of a major speech made by President Reagan:

Stripped of rhetoric, the paramount American interest in the Middle East is to prevent the region from falling under the domination of the Soviet Union. Were Moscow, or even its radical allies in the region, allowed to establish dominance or acquire a stranglehold on the West's sources of petroleum, either at the wellhead or at various oil route chokepoints, the economies of the major industrial states would be jeopardized and the capacity of NATO and Japan to resist Soviet pressure would be dangerously impaired. Indeed, any American government which allowed oil supplies to its allies to be placed in question would almost certainly invite the neutralization of Western Europe and Japan, the encirclement of China, and —eventually—its own isolation.

The critical importance of the Middle East to American global interests should be obvious, and yet the policies of our government continue the gradual erosion of our influence and power in the region. Today, the Soviet Union is capitalizing on a vast military buildup by raising the level of risk in accordance with its perception of the strategic balance. The Soviet fleet now has the run of the Mediterranean, free access to the Indian Ocean and the Persian Gulf, and is extending its global reach.

This assertion of Soviet military power at both ends of the Middle East is evident in their string of bases and naval facilities in Iraq, Syria, South Yemen, Ethiopia and Libya. The armies of all these countries are largely dependent on Soviet equipment. The recent turmoil in Iran, Afghanistan, and Turkey—all bordering upon the Soviet Union—is ominous. Each of these non-Arab states is crucial to the balance of power between the Soviet Union and the West, and in each case chaos means a gain for the Kremlin and deficit for American interests.

Meanwhile, the U.S. record is one of understatement and miscalculation regarding the extent of Soviet capabilities and Soviet interest in affecting or controlling the flow of oil from the Middle East, in base rights and in defense pacts. Swayed by the misleading abstraction of "detente," our policymakers have yet to achieve a clear understanding of the Soviet role in the region. Moscow's objectives and intentions continue to be viewed as opportunistic and not as an integral part of a major effort to alter the global balance of power.

The Iranian debacle is the most recent example of the extent to which U.S. indecision and ignorance of the challenge we face in the region obscure the true stakes. Continued instability fueled by our policies provides important opportunities to the Soviets to expand their sphere of influence and to deny or control oil resources vital to the Western economies. Meanwhile, those leaders in the area who have cast their fate with the United States now seriously question our political judgment and our ability and willingness to back our friends and to withstand threats to their survival. These developments, coupled with Brezhnev's unilateral public warning not to intervene in Iran, would indicate that the Soviet Union—not the United States—is poised to fill the power void left "East of Suez" by the British.

The Carter Administration has yet to grasp that in this region conflict and tension are endemic, a condition traceable largely to the fragmented sectarian nature of Middle Eastern society. For example, territorial disputes among Arab states are persistent; ethnic and religious rivalries abound; conservative and radical attitudes regarding social change are continuously in conflict. The recent tragedy of the Lebanese civil war and the border war between the two Yemens in 1979 are two cases in point. Thus, the more critical issues dividing Arab states actually have little to do with Israel, even though the Jewish state has served as a convenient polemical rallying point in internal Arab conflict.

The existence of Israel has served as a convenience for the Soviet Union as well, but Russian aims for control over the entire region existed long before Israel's birth in 1948. Without this bastion of liberal democracy in the heart of the area, the Kremlin would be confined to supporting militant regimes against pro-American conservative governments which would not be able to divert the attention and energies of the radicals away from themselves by using the "lightning rod" of the "Zionist State." Moreover, our own position would be weaker without the political and military assets Israel provides. Yet, American policymakers downgrade Israel's geopolitical importance as a stablizing force, as a deterrent to radical hegemony and as a military offset to the Soviet Union.

The fall of Iran has increased Israel's value as perhaps the only remaining strategic asset in the region on which the United States can truly rely; other pro-Western states in the region, especially Saudi Arabia and the small Gulf kingdoms, are weak and vulnerable. Israel's strength derives from the reality that her affinity with the West is not dependent on the survival of an autocratic or capricious ruler. Israel has the democratic will, national cohesion, technological capacity and military fiber to stand forth as America's trusted ally.

With a democratic political system like our own, we need have no fear of Israel's political stability or of the rise of a radical, anti-American leadership at her helm. Her intelligence services provide critical guidance to ongoing regional development, the technical know-how of her specialists could be used to service American equipment in a crisis, and her facilities and airfields could provide a secure point of access if required at a moment of emergency. Further, Soviet planners must constantly take into account the effective dominance of the Israeli forces and especially its air force, over critical zones of access and transit in the region. In a moment of crisis the knowledge that this air force can create a zone of danger and uncertainty to the U.S.S.R. must greatly restrict Soviet options and thereby facilitate the tasks of American planners.

Specific Arab states such as Egypt—friendly to us at a particular moment—may well be able and prepared to take a front-line position in defense of Western security interests. To the extent that one or more can participate, so much the better; but such secondary links cannot substitute for a strong Israel in the ever-turbulent Middle East.

Therefore, it is foolhardy to risk weakening our most critical remaining regional strategic asset. Yet, if administration policies should serve to weaken Israel either through building the basis for a radical Palestinian state on her borders or through providing her with insufficient military assistance, the tasks of Kremlin planners dealing with the Middle East would be enormously eased and a determined barrier to Soviet expansionism in the region would have been withdrawn.

Only by full appreciation of the critical role the State of Israel plays in our strategic calculus can we build the foundation for thwarting Moscow's designs on territories and resources vital to our security and our national well-being.

When Mr. Reagan gives his assurance to Israel that the USA and he personally are devoted to the survival of Israel I do not question his sincerity. However, if I were an Israeli and any U.S. President said, "Trust me, I will protect you," I think I would be prone to say, "Should I trust you like your South Vietnamese allies trusted the USA? Where are they now? Should we trust you like your Taiwanese allies have trusted the USA and faithfully worked for your interest in the Far East, who now see themselves being abandoned in favor of detente with Red China?"

Why should Jordan now be rewarded for over thirty years of rejectionism, war against Israel and refusal to negotiate? Why not suggest to Jordan that they make a peace treaty with Israel, following Egypt's example, and then begin to negotiate other issues that must be dealt with?

Why should Jews not be allowed to live in Biblical Judea and Samaria? God's intention is clear. His Word declares that the sons of Ishmael will live in the midst of their brethren (the Israelites). The 500,000 Israeli Palestinian Arabs (who live in the pre-1967 borders) did not flee and become refugees in 1948. They are full citizens, vote, have representation in the Israeli parliament, and enjoy the benefits of Israeli citizenship. This proves that co-existence is possible.

How we hoped that President Reagan would be the man to sponsor a new and attainable aspect of Middle East peace. It was our dream that he would seize the opportunity, as Carter did in negotiating the Egypt-Israel peace treaty and promote the rebuilding of Lebanon, then the making of a peace treaty between a free Lebanon and Israel. Mr. Begin optimistically told us that this was what he was hoping for (before Reagan's speech).

SHOULD ISRAEL GIVE AWAY JUDEA AND SAMARIA?

I once suggested to Mr. Begin that Israel should give away the West Bank (Judea and Samaria). He looked shocked that I would say this, for he knows my sentiments. I continued by saying, "You should give away Judea and Samaria when the older, more stable nations give up their occupied territories. Let the USA and the USSR lead the way. Let them set the example. LET RUSSIA WITHDRAW. Think of all the occupied territories the Russians could get out of! In just sixty years Russia has absorbed or now dominates an impressive list of occupied lands."

CAPTIVE NATIONS

Armenia*	1920	East Germany	1949
Azebaijan*	1920	Mainland China	1949
Byelorussia	1920	Tibet	1951
Cossackia	1920	Mongolia	1924
Georgia	1920	Estonia*	1940
Udel-Ural*	1920	Latvia*	1940
North Caucasia*	1920	Lithuania*	1940
Ukraine*	1920	Albania	1946
Far Eastern Republic*	1922	Bulgaria	1946
Turkestan*	1922	North Vietnam	1954
Yugoslavia	1946	Cuba	1960
Poland	1947	Cambodia	1975
Rumania	1947	South Vietnam	1975
Czechoslovakia	1948	Laos	1975
North Korea	1948	Afghanistan	1980
Hungary	1949		

*Countries absorbed into U.S.S.R.

By no means is this the end of Russia's imperial expansionism. No communist leader has ever repudiated the Marxist-Leninist ideals of total world conquest. Before demanding Israel's withdrawal from Biblical Judea and Samaria let the "northern bear" retreat to his cave and hibernate.

UNITED STATES OF AMERICA OCCUPIED TERRITORIES

Let the USA withdraw from its occupied territories taken by conquest in our previous history. Let the United States disengage from all the territories (including Texas and a lot more) seized from Mexico in 1848. Then let the U.S. pull back from the "Northwest Bank" grabbed by zealots chanting "manifest destiny." Return the Florida territories. In fact, evacuate all the illegal settlements outside the territory of the original thirteen colonies. Perhaps all Americans whose families arrived here before 1776 would be allowed to remain. Justice for the Indians at last. Finally, let New York become an internationalized city, being the seat of the United Nations world body. A simpler solution would be for all who are not American Indians to leave the USA.

Then Israel might be asked to withdraw from the Biblical territories of Judea and Samaria.

I do not wish to condemn President Reagan. I have too much love and respect for him. I just want to ask him: "Mr. President, where are you leading our nation? As a Christian I cannot accept a sell-out of Israel. I plead with you to reconsider the whole situation. I urge you to examine the Biblical mandates for the area known as the Middle East."

There ARE SOLUTIONS to the problems of the area. Here is a course of action we would suggest:

A PLAN FOR MIDEAST PEACE

1. Let Israel's neighbors recognize her right to exist. It is refusal to do this that has caused trouble in the Middle East. We need to abandon the concept that the Palestinian

problem is the root of the controversy. Let Israel be recognized and the Palestinian plight can be dealt with.

2. Let peace treaties with Israel be signed by neighboring nations.

3. Let negotiations of the Palestinian and all other problems of the Mideast then take place. Let there be no predetermined outcome, no laying down of conditions superimposed by any outside power. Let the negotiations begin with full recognition that there will be disagreement and even anger. But let the anger be expressed with words and diplomacy, not with bullets and bombs. Keep strong the hope that solutions will be found, and that peace will come to the Middle East.

17

LEBANON IN PROPHECY

The following is an article by Jan Willem van der Hoeven, Chief spokesperson, International Christian Embassy of Jerusalem:

The enemy is the great contender against God. This is seen in the fact that those individuals of nations God has chosen to play a special part in the fulfillment of His Word, are often subject to the fiercest attacks.

Among the nations, Israel is the clearest example of this truth. No nation in the world has been tried, attacked and resisted by the evil one so much as this supreme instrument among the nations of God's redemptive plan for all mankind.

The degree of attacks correspond with the degree of blessings that is intended to flow through the channel.

The wanton destruction of Lebanon, destined to be an agent of redemption for God in the entire Middle East, has to be seen in the same light. As destiny is clearly stated by Isaiah (Isaiah 29:17-24, NASB):

"Is it not yet just a little while before Lebanon will be turned into a fertile field? And the fertile field will be considered as a forest? (v. 17)

"And on that day the deaf shall hear words of a book, and out of their gloom and darkness the eyes of the blind shall see. (v. 18)

"For the ruthless will come to an end, and the scorner will be finished, indeed all who are intent in doing evil will be cut off: (v. 20)

"Who cause a person to be indicted by a word, and ensnare him who adjudicates at the gate, and defraud the one in the right with meaningless arguments. (v. 21)

"Therefore thus says the Lord, who redeemed Abraham, concerning the house of Jacob, 'Jacob shall not be ashamed, nor shall his face now turn pale: (v. 22)

"But when he sees his children, the work of My hands, in his midst, they will sanctify My name: Indeed, they will sanctify the Holy One of Jacob, and will stand in awe of the God of Israel. (v. 23)

"And those who err in mind will know the truth, and those who criticize will accept instruction.' " (v. 24)

Jan Willem van der Hoeven and his wife Widad—a Christian-Arab lady who loves Israel.

There are three things, here spoken of, in relation to Lebanon:

1. God intends to use Lebanon as His fruitful field of blessing at revival (verses 17 thru 19).

2. God will end the usurpation of the ruthless (terrorists) and scorners in Lebanon (verses 20 thru 21).

3. And all of this will lead to the copulation of His purpose in Israel and the spiritual awakening there, as is stated in Isaiah (verses 22 thru 24).

Even as in the days of King Solomon, when there was peace between Lebanon (King Hiram) and Israel through that peaceful relationship, much of the building material of the temple came to Jerusalem in the form of workers and cedars from Lebanon. So also the blessing that God will give to Lebanon will spill over to become a comfort and blessing in the building up of Zion, as the Lord had designed. As was prophesied by the mouth of Isaiah:

"The glory of Lebanon will come to you, the juniper, the box tree, and the cypress together, to beautify the place of My sanctuary; and I shall make the place of My feet glorious" (Isaiah 60:13, NASB).

AN UNUSUAL PROPHECY

In February 1982, we had a tour group visiting Israel. It was our privilege to tour north Israel. We went to the northern-most town of Metullah where we stood at the "good neighbor fence." While there we were visited by Grant Livingston who lives in nearby Kiryat Shemona. Grant is a Christian minister who lives in Israel. He began to read many Scriptures about Lebanon (including Isaiah 10:34; 29:17-24; Jeremiah 22:20-21 and others). He then began to speak prophetically saying, *"Soon Israel will invade and liberate Lebanon. Lebanon will suffer for she has not made peace with Israel, but in His mercy, God will liberate her. Then Lebanon will become the center for Gospel activity and outreach in the entire Middle East."*

Grant Livingston speaks on the prophetic significance of Lebanon at the Good Neighbor Fence—Mettulah, Israel at Lebanese border.

As we view the present situation in the Mideast, we pray that this prophecy will be fulfilled in its entirety. Perhaps our missionaries will be allowed to return to Lebanon. This time I pray that the missionaries will teach the Lebanese the truth of God's Word concerning Israel's place in prophecy and the plan of God. Perhaps the missionaries can cease their anti-Israel stance. I hope all Christians will read *The Liberated Palestinian—the Anis Shorrosh Story* (Victor Books, SP Publications, Inc., Wheaton, Illinois 60187). Also note our book review of *Jesus, Prophecy and the Middle East* by Dr. Shorrosh.

18

MAGOG, ARMAGEDDON AND THE PEACE OF JERUSALEM

Many Bible scholars foresee a very dark time, not only for the Middle East but for the whole world. An antichrist (the beast of Revelation) will force a false peace treaty on Israel. It will be for a stated duration of seven years. For a full eschatological inquiry into these matters see **THINGS TO COME** by Dr. J. Dwight Pentecost (Published by Zondervan in Grand Rapids, MI 49506).

The Bible says that when men shall say "peace and safety" then comes sudden destruction upon them. Add to this the words of Jesus as He laments a continuing condition of "wars and rumors of wars."

The beast will break the covenant and persecute Israel. Wrath is meted out on the heads of all men on the earth. Some see the church as having been taken out (raptured) previously. Others say the church will be here but supernaturally protected.

NOT PROMOTERS OF ARMAGEDDON

God did not call us to be promoters of Armageddon. We are followers of the Prince of Peace. As far as it lies within us we are to create peaceable conditions in our lives, families, nations and our world as long as we are here. God's restraining force is holding the powers of antichrist at bay.

Jesus was not gloating when He spoke of "wars and rumors of wars." He was weeping over man's rejection of His love and purpose. He was lamenting the deep inability of man to solve so many of his problems, all the while rejecting God's solutions.

Yes, the Armageddon will come in its time. We do not know when that will be, but as long as we are here may God grant that we may be people of His peace and purpose. We are to pray for the peace of Jerusalem. Anything worth praying for is worth working for. James tells us, "faith without works is dead."

There are always date-setters among us who are sure that it is about to happen. This is nothing new. It is a phenomena that continues from the time of the early church. Of course we know we are living in the "end times" and the "final era." The existence of Israel, as a fulfillment of prophecy is the one great proof of that fact. But who knows how long we will be here before the trumpet sounds? All date-setting systems are bound to fail regardless of how many followers they have. Jesus said that no one could know the day and the hour. Theologically it can be shown that this refers to the "rapture" and not the revelation/second coming at the end of the seven years of trouble. How fruitless it is to try and figure out the time of His coming. On the other hand, what a blessing it is to be busy about His work in the Kingdom right here and now.

A study of prophecy, rightly undertaken, does not promote escapism, defeatism, or irresponsibility. It is a call to be a participant in the ongoing plan and purpose of God. We are laborers together with the Lord (not hirelings but partners). God is not looking for spectators, He is looking for workers. Some day you wish to stand before God and hear Him say, "WELL DONE," (not well thought out) "thou good and faithful servant, enter thou into the joy of thy Lord."

BELIEF WITHOUT ACTION IS DECEPTION

Yes, shocking isn't it? BELIEF WITHOUT ACTION

IS DECEPTION. This is simply a restatement of James 1:22: "Be ye doers of the Word, and not hearers only, deceiving your own selves." Add to this the fact that "faith without works is dead," and you see that God's Word is a call to activism and not passivity. Too long we have allowed servants of the antichrist spirit to be the activists. It is time to sound a clarion call to the true believers to become active in the affairs of this very time in which we live.

19

CHRISTIANS UNITED
FOR ISRAEL

(Christian Organizations that Support Israel)

On 4 July 1975 an ad hoc committee of nine clergymen met and formed CHRISTIANS UNITED FOR ISRAEL. David Lewis convened the meeting and is recognized as the founder and has served until now as the president of CUFI.

CUFI has undertaken many activities, and publishes the **JERUSALEM COURIER AND PROPHECY DIGEST,** quarterly. A monthly newsletter is sent to those who are the partners of this ministry.

CUFI sponsors two tours to Israel each year, including an annual tour during the Feast of Tabernacles. Tour participants are given opportunity to meet the people as well as view the sights in the Holy Land. For information on the tours write: CHRISTIANS UNITED FOR ISRAEL, 304 East Manchester, Springfield, MO 65807.

National Christian Leadership Conference for Israel

David Lewis, president as of June 1982, was one of the original founders and incorporaters. Bill Hater is secretary-treasurer. Isaac Rottenberg, executive director, runs the New York office and does most of the hard work.

NCLCI is a coalition of organizations that are supportive of Israel. All support-Israel groups are welcome to affiliate. It provides a united front on this single issue. No doctrinal agreement is required on any other issue. This group includes leaders from every segment of the church. Information on this may be addressed to: NCLCI, 134 East 39th Street, New York, NY 10016.

NCLCI is recognized as the most effective organization of its kind, and its influence is growing.

International Christian Embassy of Jerusalem
Johann Luckhoff is the director. Jan Willem Van der Hoeven, is chief spokesperson. Joan McWhirter (Jerusalem editor of the **JERUSALEM COURIER**) is the minister of education. Merv and Merla Watson head up the ministry of fine and performing arts. There are approximately thirty other persons on the staff of the Embassy in Jerusalem.

In North America counsulates are opening in many cities. The executive director for North America is Jim Jackson. The board of directors is comprised of three men: Jamie Buckingham, Morris Sheets and David Lewis. For information you may write:

International Christian Embassy
10 Brenner Street
Jerusalem, Israel

United States Christian Embassy, Israel
P.O. Box 1000
Montreat, North Carolina 28757

Many Other Organizations
I have mentioned the above three organizations because I am deeply involved in all three and hence know more about them. There are many other fine organizations—the list is not complete. We are learning about new groups every week. I do not personally know a lot about some of these organizations. Listing them is not a recommendation, it is for reference purposes to strengthen the network of information and interaction.

International Christian Embassy Jerusalem, United States of America and Canadian Organizations Active in Support of Israel

Action Reconciliation/Service
for Peace
c/o Interaction Center
4920 Piney Branch Road, NW
Washington, DC 20011

Ad Hoc Committee for a
Unified Jerusalem
354 Lakeville Road
Lake Success, NY 11020

Rev. David Aller
Route 2
Duxbury, VT 05676

Ms. Ilana Artman
America-Israel Friendship
League
134 East 39th Street
New York, NY 10016

Association Quebec-Israel
1310 Avenue Greene
Montreal, Quebec H3Z 2B2
Canada

Rev. Jim Bakker
Jim Bakker Show
Charlotte, NC 28279

Bayshore United
Methodist Ch.
3909 South MacDill
Tampa, FL 33608

Mrs. Mary Rose Black
Calif. Christian Com. for Israel
3011 College Avenue
Berkeley, CA 94705

Rev. Ray Block
Iowans for Israel
P.O. Box 316
Webster City, IA 50595

R.J. Bommarito
Israel's Allies
P.O. Box 1028
Southfield, MI 48075

Rev. Ralph Brostrom
Midwest Christian Com. for
Israel
8881 Irving Avenue South
Minneapolis, MN 55431

Rev. Robert Bullock
New England Com. of Clergy &
Laity Concerned for Israel
59 Cottage Street
Sharon, MA 02267

Dr. Israel Carmona
38 Brook Hollow Drive
Santa Ana, CA 92705

Mrs. Mary Carse
Vermont Christians for Israel
c/o Mary's Garden
Hinnesburg, VT 05461

Mr. John Chambers
Christian Friends of Israel
5310 NW Lincoln
Topeka, KS 66618

Mr. John E. Chalmers
Christ. Friends of Israel
4225 Emland Apt. 4
Topeka, KS 66606

Christian-Israel Friendship
League
P.O. Box 400
Paradise, CA 95969

Concerned Women for America
P.O. Box 20376
El Cajon, CA 92021

Mr. David Cravit
Action Israel for
Mutual Security
180 Duncan Mill Road
Suite 300
Don Mills, Ontario M3B 1Z6
Canada

Rev. Harold Dart
Int'l Assoc. of Christians
for Israel
P.O. Box 4080
Bellingham, WA 98225

Mr. Joe Dean
Christians for Israel
P.O. Box 1730
Newport Beach, CA 92660

Rev. Roland de Corneille
Canada-Israel Parli.
Friendship Group
825 Eglington Avenue
W. Toronto, Ontario
Canada

Rev. Ric Durfield
3747 Valley Lights Drive
Pasadena, CA 91107

Rev. William Ebling
"Committee of 50"
c/o First Baptist Ch.

9603 Belmont St.
Bellflower, CA 90706

Mr. Frank Eiklor
Shalom Fellowship
P.O. Box 582
Keene, NH 03431

Mr. Mike Evans
Lovers of Israel
P.O. Box 61999
Dallas, TX 75261

Mr. Herb Fader
Gathering of Believers
Community
Washington, D.C.

Rev. Jerry Falwell
Moral Majority
500 Allegheny Avenue
Lynchburg, VA 24501

Rev. Dr. Robert G. Grant
Christian Voice
P.O. Box 415
Pacific Grove, CA 93950

Mr. Keith Grimes
10104 Castile Road
Richmond, VA 23233

Rev. John Hagee
"A Night to Honor Israel"
214 Roleto Drive
San Antonio, TX 78213

Mr. J. Heintz
Peace for Israel
P.O. Box 8311
Pembroke Pines, FL 33024

Mr. Gilman Hill
6200 Plateau Drive
Englewood, CO 80111

Mr. & Mrs. R.E. Hoefle
Epiphany Bib. Students
Association
P.O. Box 97
Mount Dora, FL 32757

Rev. Robert Hooley
Faith Bible Chapel
6210 Ward Road
Arvada, CO 80004

House of David
P.O. Box 777, Dept. A
Lakewood, NY 14750

Mrs. Lesli A. Hromas
Two Quail Ridge South
Rolling Hills, CA 90274

Rev. H. Jacoba Hurt
Christian Brides to Israel
3456 Fraser Street
Vancouver, B.C. V5V 4C4
Canada

Intercessors for America
P.O. Box D
Elyria, OH 44035

International Christians for
Israel
P.O. Box 873
La Mirada, CA 90637

Jewish-Christian Com. for
Israel
2217 Montrose, Suite 200
Houston, TX 77006

Mr. Vendyl Jones
Instit. of Judaic-Christian
Research
P.O. Box 35
Tyler, TX 75710

Rev. Elmer Josephson
Bible Light International
P.O. Box E
Hillsboro, KS 67063

Mrs. Elva Lanowick
Christian-Israel Friendship
League
P.O. Box 400
Paradise, CA 95969

Mr. Howard Leighton-Floyd
Support Israel
Anderson, MO 64831

Mrs. Yvonne Lewerke
Iowa Christian Friends
of Israel
1005 S. 15 Street
Clear Lake, IA 50428

Mr. Edward McAteer
The Roundtable
1500 Wilson Blvd., Suite 502
Arlington, VA 22209

Sister Margaret McGrath
Centre Mi-ca-el
4661 Queen Mary Road
Montreal, Quebec
Canada

Ministries of Vision
P.O. Box 4130
Medford, OR 97501

Original Gospel Movement
3721 80 Street
Jackson Heights
New York, NY 10002

Dr. Frank Oerth
N.E. Com. for Israel
858 Great Plain Avenue
Needham, MA 02161

Dr. Arnold T. Olson
Evang. Free Ch. of America
1515 East 66 Street
Minneapolis, MN 55423

Mr. George Otis
High Adventure Ministries
P.O. Box 7466
Van Nuys, CA 91409

Mr. Raymond Oram
The Friends of Israel
475 White Horse Pike
West Collingwood, NJ 08107

Rev. Jim Parker
308 Elmwood Lane
Williamsburg, VA 23185

Reconcilliation Fellowship
P.O. Box 40867
Washington, D.C. 20016

Mr. Derek Prince
Shiloh Fellowship
P.O. Box 14252
Fort Lauderdale, FL 33302

Dr. David Reagan
Lamb and Lion Ministries
P.O. Box 527
Plano, TX 75074

Rev. James Robison
J.R. Evang. Association
P.O. Box 18489
Fort Worth, TX 76118

Mr. Randy Rott
Box 10379
Kansas City, MO 64111

Rev. Rayard Rustin
Black Americans to Support
Israel Committee
260 Park Avenue South
New York, NY 10010

Mr. George Samson
Evang. United for Zion
P.O. Box 68
Lakehurst, NJ 08733

Mr. Matthew Schwartz
Intercessors for Israel
11125 College Street
Kansas City, MO 64137

Mrs. Gwen Shaw
End Time Handmaidens, Inc.
P.O. Box 447
Jasper, AR 72641

Mr. Douglas Shearer
TAV Evang. Ministries
P.O. Box 281
Elverta, CA 95626

Rev. Morris Sheats
P.O. Box 635
Mansfield, TX 76063

Rev. Bob Shelley
3909 South McDill
Tampa, FL 33611

Rev. Peter Sluys
Canadian Friends of
New Ammin
Route 3
Salmon Arms. B.C.
Canada

Andy Sorrell
800 Bering Room 202
Houston, TX 77003

Rev. Thomas Stewart
American Friends of
Nes Ammin
724 Delaware Avenue
Buffalo, NY 14209

Rev. Hilton Sutton
Mission to America
736 Wilson Road
Humble, TX 77338

Jack van Impi Ministries
Box J
Royal Oak, MI 48068

Bridges for Peace
Box 33145
Tulsa, OK 74135

Mr. Wally Wenge
P.O. Box 819
Kaiua Kona
Hawaii 96740